Secretarial Procedures Applied

Helen Harding

Pitman

PITMAN PUBLISHING LIMITED
128 Long Acre, London WC2E 9AN

Associated Companies
Pitman Publishing Pty Ltd, Melbourne
Pitman Publishing New Zealand Ltd, Wellington

© Helen Harding 1985

First published in Great Britain 1985

British Library Cataloguing in Publication Data
Harding, Helen
    Secretarial procedures applied.
    1. Secretaries—Problems, exercises, etc.
    2. Office practice—Problems, exercises, etc.
    I. Title
    651.3'741'076   HF5547.5

Typeset 10/12 pt Baskerville and printed in Great Britain
at The Pitman Press, Bath

ISBN 0 273 01918 X

Contents

Preface

Secretarial Procedures Applied has been developed to accompany my more theoretical *Secretarial Procedures*, which is, therefore, recommended reading if maximum benefit is to be gained from this text.

The structure and format of the units in this activity book reflect the sequence used in the theory text. Taken together they represent a new and comprehensive approach to the study and application of this subject.

For whom is the book designed?

The book is designed to cater for students preparing for a range of examinations but principally for the following:

RSA   Secretarial Duties Stage II
LCCI   Office Organisation and Secretarial Procedures (Private Secretary's Certificate)
PEI   Secretarial Practice Intermediate

However, it will also serve as a foundation for the more advanced qualifications of these examining bodies in that a deeper and more mature treatment can be given to many of the situations devised within the units. It will also provide useful material for more practically-based courses like BTEC Secretarial Modules, or for non-examinable refresher courses where evaluation is by continuous assessment.

How is it put together?

The book comprises four parts, each with a distinct flavour and purpose.

Part I offers guidelines on learning to study effectively in the form of advice on study techniques and the acquisition of essential study skills.

Part II consists of twelve units based on specific objectives. The units are designed to help students apply theoretical knowledge and understanding to a variety of tasks such as they can expect to find both in situation-based examination questions and when they commence their secretarial careers.

Part III is made up of crossword puzzles designed with revision in mind. Some of the clues are very obvious whilst others offer more challenge, but all the answers are to be found within *Secretarial Procedures*.

Part IV offers advice on examinations – how to prepare for them and how to realise full potential on the day.

How might it best be used?

The combination of theory and practice is always essential if learning is to prove worthwhile and meaningful. This book is, therefore, intended for use in conjunction with *Secretarial Procedures*. On its own it does not provide the answers but rather poses the problems in the form of situation-based tasks of varying degrees of length and difficulty.

It may be used effectively by students for personal study, but is ideally suited as a class text where students can benefit from shared experience and the guidance offered by the tutor. Whatever the situation, it is essential to enter into the spirit of the activities and to visualise oneself in the situations described. This requires flexibility and imagination – two qualities which all potential secretaries are expected to possess! Only when individuals let the actor or actress in them loose for the purposes of the scenario presented will they get the best out of the questions and arrive at the most likely and acceptable solutions. Likewise, the issues explored will become more realistic when different perspectives are considered and different views put forward for discussion.

In conclusion

My intention in writing this book has been to provide a selection of material and ideas to actively support my theory text. Obviously it is impossible to satisfy every criterion, particularly when one is catering for a range of examinations; thus not all the material will prove useful to everyone. However, what I hope readers will do is to find the germ of an idea which appeals and which they can then adapt to suit their own purposes. For instance, certain of the activities may be too long or too complex for certain groups, but there is no reason why bits cannot be used as needs arise and time permits. Conversely, it may be desired to develop themes or suggestions much further than I have – and why not indeed? This is surely what effective practical activity is all about.

You will notice that I have favoured suggesting topics for discussion in the group activities sections, and this has been a deliberate strategy on my part. Given that secretarial duties, practice or procedures – call it what we will – is firmly based on situations encountered by secretaries working in business, I make no apology for this. It is only by providing ample opportunity to communicate, use judgement and exercise interpersonal skills and abilities that students will be adequately prepared both for examinations and, possibly more importantly, for their future careers.

No model answers are provided within the text. In my view such an addition would discourage the creativity and original thought so essential to develop decision-making skills and foster initiative. Besides, far be it from me to put forward my views as the definitive solutions when so many of the situations used can satisfactorily be transacted, resolved or dealt with in a variety of different ways. The activities will be decidedly more meaningful in terms of the insight and experience they offer when provision is made for the exercise of imagination and when the solutions put forward are flavoured by a variety of inputs arrived at from different types of knowledge and experience.

Please be aware that any specific reference to secretaries as 'she' and bosses as 'he' within the text is purely for convenience.

However this text is ultimately used, I hope it will help to provide that all-important practical back-up which is so necessary if this subject is to be brought to life in a meaningful and acceptable way.

Above all, I should like to feel that readers will enjoy the activities set and experience a sense of achievement and satisfaction in putting their theory into practice.

Helen Harding

Part I   Learning to study effectively

Introduction

Whether you attend a class at school or college, whether you are full or part time, and no matter how old you are, effective study is something which *can* be learned. It is a matter of how you organise yourself, manage your time and marshal all available resources, often for the purpose of achieving success in that all-important examination. It goes without saying that to study well depends on your wanting to achieve success and, if an examination has to be taken, to pass and pass well. There is no room for indifference when it comes to achieving mastery over any subject. The purpose of any examination is to test your competence, skills and ability to handle questions utilising your own knowledge and judgement. Some practical suggestions as to how you might tackle revision for examinations come in Part IV, but meantime let us consider the business of studying.

Purpose of study

Many people study for examinations, at different levels and for different reasons. The study of any subject is the process of acquiring knowledge and understanding of specialised information, sometimes mainly theoretical or academic (eg history and literature), sometimes largely practical (eg catering or hairdressing) and in other instances a mixture of both, as, in fact, with the study of secretarial subjects.

So you want to study secretarial procedures? This means that you want to become an expert in this area of activity and everything it involves. The qualifications you acquire as a result of your study will indicate to prospective employers your expertise and capacity for filling the secretarial role effectively. The ultimate purpose of your studying, then, is to secure a secretarial position in pursuit of your chosen career.

Approaches to studying

Background

There are many different courses for secretaries. They operate in different ways and require different approaches even though the subject matter is largely the same. If you are to begin to study effectively you need to find out precisely what you are expected to do during your course and for the examination. Many courses for secretaries expect students to undertake and complete ongoing course work, much of which will involve the completion of in-tray exercises and the preparation and presentation of assignments of some kind. It may even be the case that your course work will contribute to your overall profile. For instance, with BTEC courses your performance in assignments during the year is taken in conjunction with your performance in the examination to establish your overall grade. Whatever the format, familiarity with the requirements is an essential first step.

Syllabuses

Always try to acquire the actual syllabus of the examining board whose qualification you are attempting to secure. Often your teacher or lecturer will ensure that you have the relevant information, but if you are in any doubt take the initiative and find out for yourself. It is a simple matter to send for details to the appropriate board. It is vital that you know what will be required of you, namely the format of the examination, its length, the subject areas covered, the element of choice (if there is one) and any special recommendations for study made by the board. Also, many boards produce reading lists and advice to candidates, and you would do well to study these at the beginning of your course.

Reading

Most, if not all, of the information you need for written aspects of your course will be found in a variety of textbooks and associated literature. Effective reading includes recognition of alternative sources as well as getting the most out of your set textbook(s). If you have been asked to obtain a particular textbook(s) be sure to do so at the beginning of your course. It is all very well to contemplate sharing with a friend or to say that there are plenty of books in the library, but you owe it to yourself and your teacher/lecturer to get your own copy of the recommended text. Library books should be viewed as supplements to your own materials, not as substitutes. Even where a set book is not prescribed you should set about choosing one which appeals to you. Many students know to their cost the risk they take by failing to secure their own books. Not only are they unable to undertake any reading preparation in advance of lessons/lectures but they will frequently find that all library copies are gone from the shelves, particularly around assignment times or near to examinations.

Techniques

Many students make the mistake of attempting to read textbooks from cover to cover, thinking that they might miss something important or even feeling that they are cheating if they only read parts! A more realistic, if not honest, approach is needed. Most textbooks seem to have a knack of putting readers to sleep very quickly, especially when approached as mammoth challenges to be read in their entirety, possibly in the few weeks leading up to the examination! Inevitably, passive, uncoordinated and unstructured reading leads to frustration, boredom and increased anxiety – particularly when you simply cannot understand and grasp the point no matter how closely or how many times you read the text.

An imaginative approach, on the other hand, pays dividends. Active rather than passive reading makes a major contribution to effective studying. Active reading is really like being a detective – finding the clues, establishing the evidence and identifying the main issues involved. Active reading is about focus, about being precise and solving problems. There seems little point in even picking up a textbook unless you want to know something or wish to substantiate a point or elaborate on some knowledge or idea you are in the process of studying.

So the practical, active approach to reading involves finding out answers to questions which are important, either in relation to course work or examination requirements or simply because you want to know. Jot down your questions and carefully study your set books and associated materials in search of the answers. Your strategy needs to be flexible. You will soon develop the skill of knowing when to skim and when to read closely and carefully.

Guidelines

The following is a well-tested technique which can be adapted to meet most reading needs. It is often referred to as SQ3R, which represents the initial letters of the *five* steps recommended in studying a book or chapter:

1 *Survey* to get the general idea of the text.
2 *Question* yourself on what you expect to get out of the reading on completion.
3 *Read* the text.
4 *Recall* (or try to recall) the main points.
5 *Review* again to check how well you have understood the main points.

The *survey of a book* should include:

• the title page
• the preface
• the contents
• the index (if there is one)
• a quick leaf through the book

The *survey of a chapter* should entail looking at:

• the first and last pages
• summaries
• headings
• any photographs, figures or diagrams
• any specimen questions

Additional points to consider

1 Always read with a sense of purpose – with questions to be answered.
2 When you read, do so initially to get a general impression and the main ideas. *Do not* make notes or underline things at this stage. This should come later when you review. Besides, your initial reactions may not be the right ones!
3 Next pick out the *important details*; sometimes this will require a second reading.
4 *Evaluate* what you are reading; look for arguments, contradictions and limitations.
5 Try to develop a faster reading speed. Most people are capable of reading half as fast again whilst still having the same degree of understanding. Practise timing yourself over selected material.
6 Try to increase your recognition span. Try to take in groups of words rather than read word by word. A good way to test your ability to do this is to read newspapers. You should be able to read column widths without scanning across the columns. Your eyes should travel down the columns and not from left to right!
7 Try not to regress whilst you are reading, ie to go over pieces in a 'looping' fashion. Most of us are guilty of this, but it slows down our reading speed immensely and is something we should try to avoid.
8 How good is your eyesight? Might you need spectacles? If you have not had your eyes tested in the last two years and think you may have eye defects make an appointment with an optician.
9 Do your lips move whilst you are reading? This is a bad habit and almost certainly means that you read slowly.
10 Build up your vocabulary. A wide vocabulary is essential for both understanding other people's ideas and better expressing your own. When you are uncertain, as to the precise meaning of a word you come across in your reading, look it up in the dictionary. It is surprising how

quickly you will encounter that same word again!

Notetaking

When you attend a lesson or lecture you should *always* be prepared to take *your own* notes, even if you know that a handout will be forth-coming. Sometimes the task will be made easier for you in that, at the beginning of the lesson or lecture, you may be supplied with an incomplete handout. This is likely to take the form of headings with blank spaces after them, and perhaps a list of suggested reading at the end. What the lecturer is really attempting to do here is to channel your thinking and concentration along his/her own lines; certainly the brief headings will be designed to follow the structures of the lecture, and as such can be a useful aid to you in making good notes. In many instances, however, the responsibility is yours and you should not shirk the task. Making notes also has the benefit of acting as an aid to concentration. If you decide to make notes you are, by the very nature of the activity, predisposed to listening to what is being said by the speaker.

Effective listening

Strange as it may seem, effective listening is something which needs to be cultivated if you are going to make useful notes. It is surprising how easy it is to *hear* without listening! In addition it is even possible to write – often in shorthand – without really listening to what is being said! How many times have you taken a full page of shorthand notes without having any real idea of what the subject was about? The same can be true of typing. How often have you typed a passage without absorbing any of the content? This is worth thinking about. Obviously human beings have an in-built capacity to operate on several levels at once. We can think we are listening when in fact we are only hearing; we are really involved in our own thoughts, which may have absolutely nothing to

do with the matter in hand. The same can be the case when taking notes.

Therefore effective studying is based on effective listening, which results in effective notetaking, which in turn depends on clarity, conciseness and consistency – the three Cs.

The three Cs

Clarity
There is little point in making notes – in either longhand or shorthand – if you cannot read them back later. This means that you need to write clearly with an appropriate pen or pencil and in a suitable notebook – not on scraps of paper which you will lose on the way home! Incomprehensible scribble is obviously hopeless, but you know best when it comes to reading your own writing or shorthand notes what counts as scribble – or you should! To be on the safe side, always transcribe at the earliest opportunity; any minute secretary will be quick to underline the value of this. Not only are you better placed to read your notes at all, but your memory will be sharper and will help you fill in the blanks or doubtful bits and elaborate on the detail.

Conciseness
Never attempt to take down everything, even where you use shorthand. Be selective. Try to develop an ability to précis the main points. Sometimes, however, it will be more useful to write down verbatim the actual words of the speaker, eg when a definition is being given, where there is a quote from a legal document or where you realise that a major explanation or insight is being offered. On other occasions it will be preferable for you to pause, listen carefully to what is being said and then jot down the main ideas expressed, using your own words.

Remember too, that everything you take down in the way of rough notes will require to be refined and transformed into logical notes that will serve as a major resource for revision at a later date.

Consistency

Consistency is essential when you transfer your notes from rough to a more structured and logical sequence. For example, always attempt to formalise your notes as quickly as possible after the lecture has taken place. Avoid building up a mass of scribbled notes which all require to be written or typed up at once! All notes should have the title of the lecture and should carry a date. Where there is more than one lecturer on the course, the appropriate name should also be added. The notes should be accompanied by any handouts given and should carry suitable references were possible. This all requires discipline on your part, but it is part of any good prospective secretary's training to develop skills in presentation, eg the use of layout, colour coding, capitalising, underscoring, indexing, presenting in a logical sequence and cross-referencing. Such techniques will greatly facilitate revision and make future reference a relatively quick and easy matter.

A personal card index

One useful addition you might consider, particularly if you are studying for an examination, is the preparation of a card index system to supplement your notes. This index would be broken down according to the syllabus headings set out by the examining board. It would be a good idea to use a coloured card for each main heading. Behind each 'leader' card would be the subdivisions or themes featured under particular topics. Take the following example:

Syllabus headings: Meetings (a coloured card)

Subdivisions might include:

- types of meeting
- documents involved
- secretary's duties
  Further subdivisions: before
  during
  after

- the chairman's role
- terminology

On each card you should summarise the main points and cross-reference them to both your own detailed notes and any textbook references you have used.

Finally you could complete each syllabus heading with a card referring to questions from past examination papers. You would indicate the examining body, the series, the year and the question number.

Time management

Effective study requires that you use your time effectively. Short, intensive study is a more efficient way of learning. You are less likely to become tired during your study sessions if you plan them on the basis of, say, three one-hour sessions, with breaks for a rest in between, rather than one session of three hours. Of course, how you organise your study time is a personal decision and depends to a large extent on your own preferences. Some students prefer to 'burn the midnight oil' whilst others adopt a more casual approach. The rest of us fall somewhere between these two extremes and therefore need a plan of campaign. Any plan will also need to take into account things like your home circumstances, ie whether you have a room of your own and whether the house is quiet for studying. It may be that you find it preferable to study somewhere else like a library. Even so you still need to be organised so that you can make the best use of your time.

It is often a good idea to manage your study time on the basis of a carefully worked out timetable in order to establish a routine of study. Be sure to be realistic when drawing up such a timetable. There is little point in producing a personal study programme (PSP) which includes two hours or so on an evening when you like to watch a favourite television programme! The more genuine your PSP the more likely you will be able to stick to it, thus giving your confidence a boost every time you complete a week according to plan.

To decide whether your own PSP reflects effective time management depends on a positive response to the following questions, which I would like you to consider once you have devised your PSP:

1 Do you have a well-thought-out (ie realistic) plan of campaign which takes into account your social and leisure activities as well as school/college holidays?
2 Are you working to short intensive study sessions centred on the achievement of specific study objectives?
3 Have you decided when to study? Are you freshest in the morning, or is the evening better for you? Choose the time when you can maximise your efforts.
4 Have you decided how to pace your PSP? Clearly you need a programme suited to the particular demands of your course. Be flexible. If you are given a lecture it is a good idea to intensify your own studies immediately, or as soon as possible, afterwards. On the other hand, if you know that you are going to be involved in a series of group discussions, then it makes sense to prepare (ie study) *before* these take place.
5 Have you decided where to study and what study aids you will need to use?

If you can answer 'yes' to these five questions then you are well on your way to managing your study time effectively. If on the other hand you experience difficulty in being positive, then you need to think again. Always remember that studying is a personal activity and depends on you organising yourself in such a way as to achieve a balance which suits your needs and circumstances.

Summary

This part of the book – on learning to study effectively – is of necessity somewhat brief. My intention has been to provide you with insight into what studying involves and to offer guidelines on how you can realistically go about acquiring the necessary skills. Remember, too, that the ability to study is an acquired discipline, governed by the strength of your own will and your commitment to succeed. It is not something you are born with but it can be learned.

In addition I have tried to encourage you to think constructively about your present study techniques with a view to modifying and adapting them to meet new demands and differing circumstances.

There is no conclusion to be reached or final statement to be made about the art of studying, since it is a lifelong process.

Part II Study units

Introduction

This part comprises twelve units which provide a means of applying the knowledge and understanding gleaned from the study of *Secretarial Procedures* via a series of tasks and activities, many of which are situation based.

Each unit follows a set pattern. A broad *general aim* is followed by a series of *specific objectives* which students should be able to attain on completion of the unit. Then come the following sections.

Self-testing warm-up

In order to assess readiness to tackle the activities, each unit contains a selection of short revision questions on which students should test themselves as a warm-up to the real 'meat' of the unit's activities. If difficulties are experienced in answering these warm-up questions, students are advised to return to the theory text and reread necessary parts before progressing further.

Situation-based activities

In keeping with many current examination formats, the tasks which follow are located in a briefly described situation. The intention is to encourage realistic application to the exercises and problems set, and to provide a background from which students may work and expand their ideas to provide more meaningful solutions. Some of the activities require merely that the student undertakes one major activity, whilst others involve a series of related tasks which may be tackled in their entirety or in a selective manner dependent upon the requirements of the course and the relevance to the theory sessions and the study which has gone before.

Personal activities

Each unit provides suggestions for practical activities which students may consider undertaking. The pursuit of even some of the suggestions put forward will certainly help supplement the material provided in the conventional sense (ie via textbooks, lectures and practical course work) and will also cause students to integrate their studies in more realistic ways. Secretarial studies should never be compartmentalised; the boundaries between subject areas are decidedly grey. It should also be possible to relate a lot of practical secretarial work to everyday activities outside school or college.

Group activities

This is an extension of the personal activities, and has been included to give students the opportunity to work together in a spirit of organised cooperation and to discuss and exchange views on issues referred to or touched on in the study unit.

1 Understanding organisations

Aim of the unit

The unit provides insight into business organisations, the way they are structured, the relationships which exist, the duties and responsibilities of executive personnel and the functions undertaken by departments.

Specific objectives

At the end of this unit you should be able to:

1 Define what is meant by 'an organisation'.
2 Differentiate between the public and private sectors.
3 Draw up and complete organisation charts.
4 Represent aspects of organisational structure in the form of a diagram.
5 Explain different types of organisation structure.
6 Identify the main advantages and disadvantages of the committee structure.
7 Explain what is meant by 'span of control'.
8 Compare and contrast the patterns of relationship which exist in large and small organisations.
9 Outline the objectives and roles of different departments.
10 Describe the duties and responsibilities of executive personnel within departments in an organisation.
11 Identify the role and function of a Secretary/Personal Assistant within the context of a large organisation.
12 Recognise why secretaries need to know about organisations.

Self-testing warm-up

1 Business organisations are basically of two types. What are they?
2 What are the principal forms of business enterprise in the private sector?
3 Give examples of nationalised industries in the UK.

4 What are the terms given to the most common forms of organisational structure in a large concern?

5 What are the advantages of a committee structure?

6 What sort of duties do Boards of Directors perform?

7 Why do large organisations have departments?

8 Suggest the principal departments you would expect to find in a manufacturing organisation.

9 What are the principal functions of a Sales Department?

10 What is the purpose of an organisation chart?

11 What are the different styles of organisation charts?

12 Compare and contrast the organisation of a large and a small business.

Situation-based activities

Situation 1

Imagine that you work for Miller & Dobson PLC whose organisation chart is outlined in Fig 1. Giving due consideration to the way in which the organisation is set out, complete the following tasks:

a Isolate, preferably with a fluorescent pen, a section of the chart which provides an example of line and staff structure in Miller & Dobson, and explain the relationships which exist in terms of authority and responsibility.

b Illustrate a strong staff relationship which is likely to exist within the organisation by marking it in a broken *red* line on the organisation chart.

c Given that Miller & Dobson are manufacturers of soaps and allied products, which sort of work would you expect to be undertaken by the Research and Development Department and what sort of personnel would you expect to find employed there?

d Outline the duties of the Company Secretary in an organisation like Miller & Dobson.

e Identify and label on the organisation chart those functions which would necessarily be controlled by experts.

f Assume that on the preparation of a new chart the position of Secretary/PA to the Managing Director would be included. On Fig 1, show how this role would be represented. Use a coloured pen please.

Situation 2

Assume that you work in the Public Relations Section of the Marketing Department of Miller & Dobson and that you are often asked to organise conducted tours for parties of visitors. These tours normally begin with a short introductory talk by someone from the Public Relations Section, continue with visits to the production lines, the Advertising Department and the Packing Section, and finish with tea in the company canteen.

Your task is to draw up a $2\frac{1}{2}$ hour programme for a party of twelve students from a local technical college and prepare a suitable handout on the work of these departments. This handout will be given to the visitors at the end of the afternoon, together with a small selection of sample products.

Situation 3

Imagine that you work in the main reception area of a medium-sized manufacturing division (concentrating on the production of three products) of a large public company. It is company policy to have a large chart illustrating the organisation of each division in the foyer of each location. During recent redecoration, the chart, which consisted of magnetic labels on a backing board, was dismantled by the cleaners and the pieces put away in a box. The Managing Director has commented on its absence and wants it restored.

a Using the outline which still exists on the

Miller & Dobson PLC

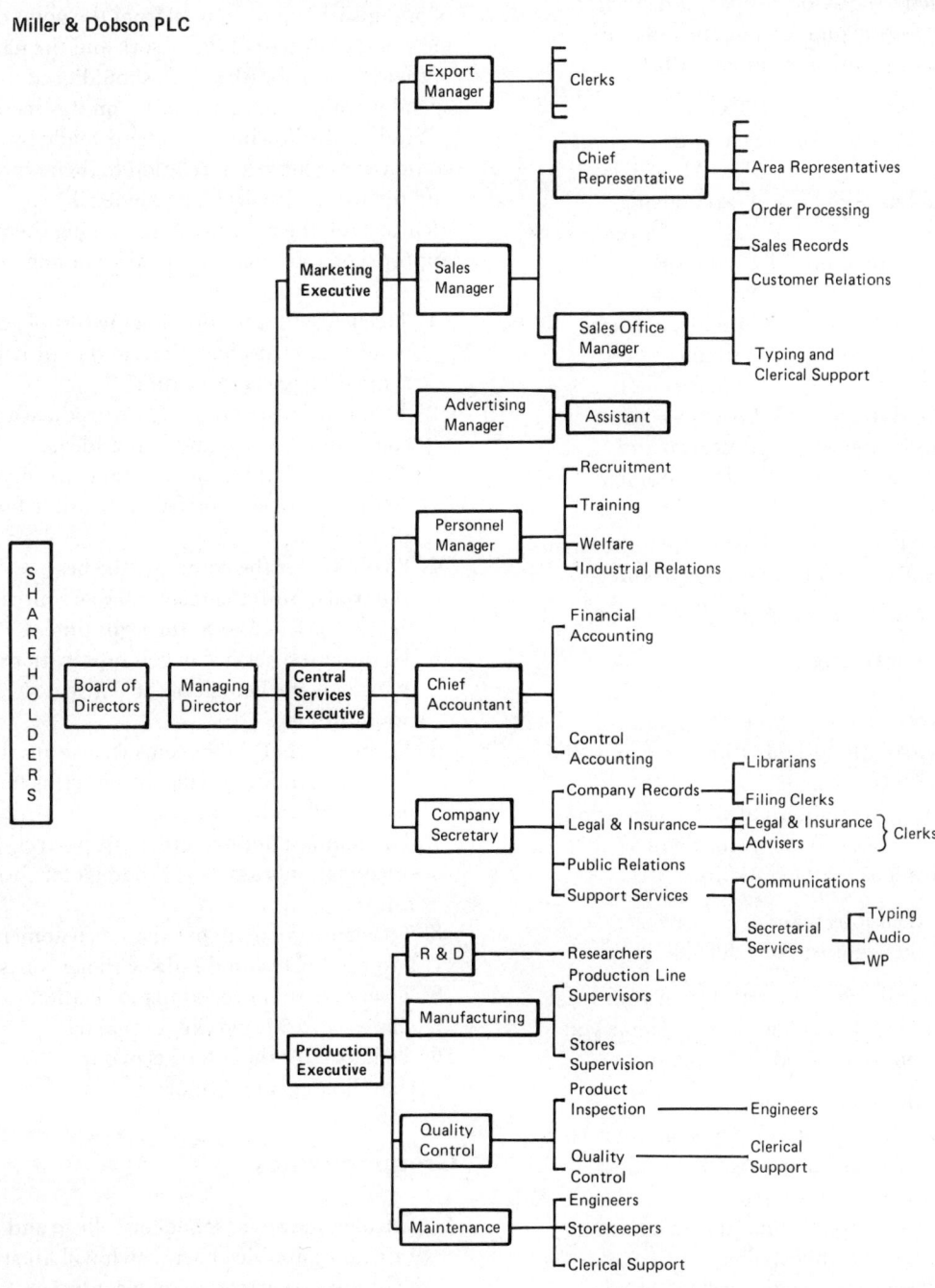

Fig 1

magnetic board, place the appropriate labels in the correct places. The actual task will be delegated to a junior. Prepare a trial chart (Fig. 2) for the junior using the following labels (which are in random order):

Sales	O & M
Product C	Accounts
Distribution	Raw Materials
General Supplies	Warehousing
Finance	Product Development
Personal Assistant	Product B
Records	Personnel
Wages	Support Services
Transport	Training
Product A	Welfare
General Manager	Overseas
Administration	Research and
Purchasing	Development
Managing Director	

b On completion of the chart suggest the 'span of control' problems which the product managers are likely to experience.

Personal activities

1 Try to obtain a selection of company handbooks and in-house literature and study the contents.
2 Interview, in an informal way, people you know who work in offices inside three different organisations. Try to establish:

   a how their jobs differ
   b how the organisations differ

3 Collect and collate material from your local press and national newspapers. Items you might consider including would be:

   a organisational problems
   b the starting up of a new business
   c the expansion of an existing business
   d the closure of a company
   e aspects of organisation reflecting a nationalised undertaking
   f aspects of organisation reflecting a government department at either national or local level

Who said it, and why?

This section is designed to test your awareness of organisational personnel from the point of view of the content of their work and the nature of their responsibilities. You should need to spend no more than 15 minutes on this section.

Study the following statements made by company executives in relation to their work and the work of their departments. Try to identify who the executives are, giving them appropriate job titles, and justify your choices.

1 To ensure that we provide the sort of goods which our customers want and to provide them in the necessary time.
2 To improve the products we produce and come up with new and better ideas.
3 To ensure that human relations within the company are as good as it is possible for them to be.
4 To obtain for the company the best materials, from the most reliable sources, at the best prices and at the right time.
5 To provide a service of communications and record for the benefit of the entire organisation.
6 To ensure that the systems we use are the most economic and effective in terms of the use of staff and resources.
7 To maintain financial records, protect the organisation's assets and budget for the future.
8 To ensure goodwill of existing customers and establish sound links with new ones.
9 To ensure that everything in relation to share registration is kept up to date.
10 To look after the interests of our shareholders at all times.

Group activities

1 Consider your own school or college and draw up a suitable chart which will illustrate the organisation, the span of control and the lines of authority and responsibility which exist.

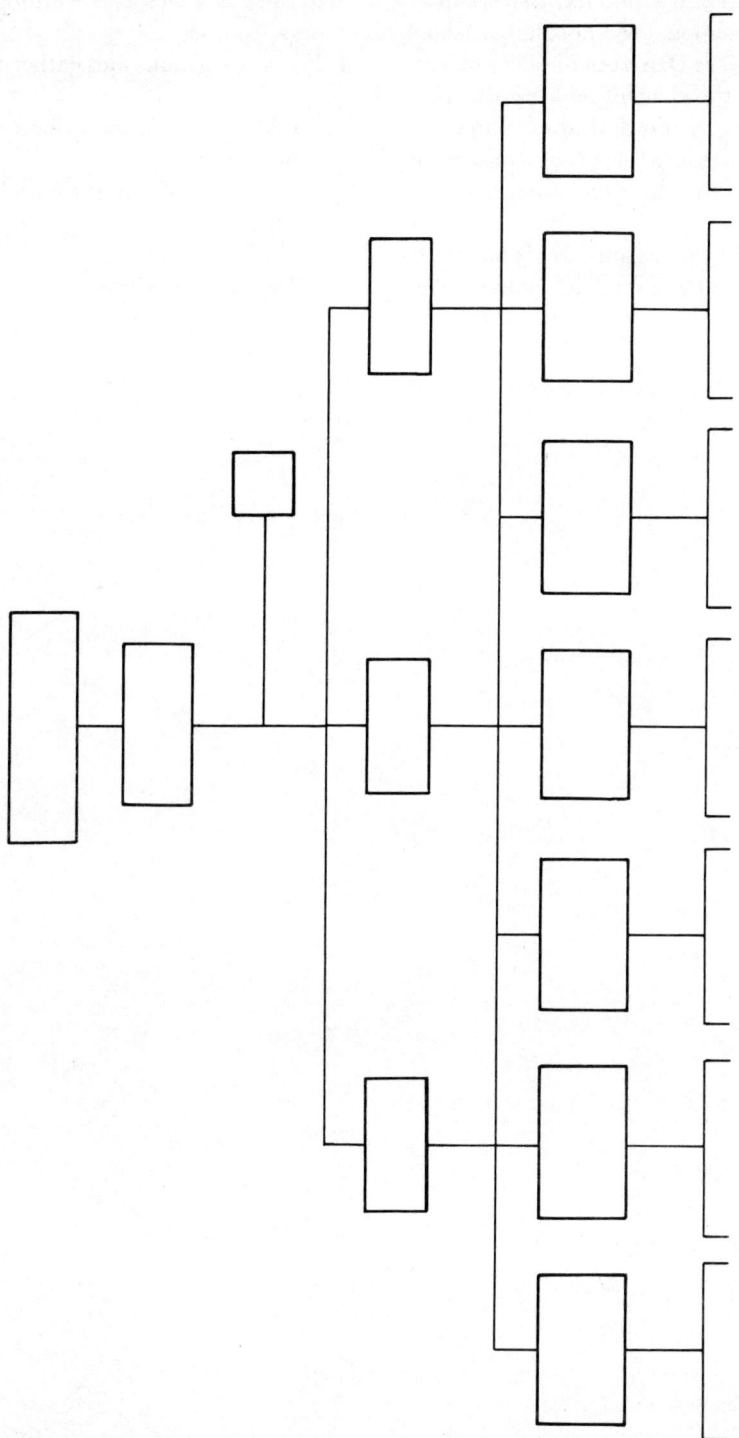

Fig 2

2 Discuss whether you would like to work in a 'people' organisation, (eg a hospital, a school, the Social Services Department of your local authority, or a travel agent) *or* a 'producing' organisation (eg the Ford Motor Company, ICI, a food processing corporation or clothing manufacturer). In your discussions justify your choice.

3 In a group, study an organisation's handbook and consider what you think it would be like to work as a secretary within that organisation.

4 Form two groups and gather material:

a in defence of working for a small organisation
b in defence of working for a large organisation

Debate your views.

2 Appreciating the office environment

Aim of the unit

The unit defines the office in the context of large and small organisations by detailing its role and function and analysing the services it provides, the members who make up its staff and the environment within which it operates.

Specific objectives

At the end of this unit you should be able to:

1 Explain the functions of the office within the organisation.
2 Describe the different office services which are likely to be performed within an organisation.
3 Explain what is meant by centralisation of services.
4 Suggest services which tend to lend themselves to centralisation.
5 Outline the advantages and disadvantages of centralisation.
6 Identify staff who work within the framework of an office.
7 Describe the duties and responsibilities of different office staff.
8 Outline the qualifications, qualities and experience looked for in office staff.
9 Comment on the importance of environment in relation to office work.
10 Draw up a detailed list of the environmental aspects which affect office working conditions.
11 Describe an open plan office.
12 Compare and constrast the office work of large and small organisations.

Self-testing warm-up

1 What are the main functions of an office within an organisation?
2 What is meant by 'centralisation of office services'?
3 Suggest activities in office work which might well be centralised.

15

4 What are the main office jobs you would expect to find in a large organisation?

5 Outline the duties and responsibilities of a Private Secretary.

6 Outline the duties and responsibilities of a Shorthand Typist.

7 Describe *three* important environmental aspects of the office.

8 Explain what you understand by the term 'modular furniture'.

9 Identify *three* specific features relating to work in a large organisation compared with work in a small company.

10 Identify *three* specific features you would expect to find when working in a small office.

Situation-based

Situation 1

Imagine that your organisation has decided to centralise all its typing and reprographic services. Up to now you have worked as Secretarial Assistant in the Sales Department, where you did all the routine typing and copying work as well as general office duties for the Department. Now you have to be moved to the Typing Pool in the Administration Block. What differences will you be likely to find, and what will be the advantages and disadvantages of such a move? Write a letter to a friend explaining the changes.

Situation 2

Imagine that you work as a shorthand typist within Miller & Dobson PLC, the company you met in Unit 1. A vacancy for a secretary is soon to come up in a solicitor's office in your home town and you are considering applying for the position.

a What differences would you expect to encounter:

   i in the nature of the work

   ii in the type of organisation

   iii in working as a secretary as opposed to a shorthand typist?

b What qualifications and qualities would you expect the firm of solicitors to look for in a successful secretary?

c You work in a large open-plan office at Miller & Dobson PLC.

   i Draw a layout of this office.

   ii State the advantages and disadvantages of working in such an environment.

   iii Describe how you expect the offices of the solicitors to compare with yours; a drawing would be helpful.

Situation 3

You work as Secretary/PA for the Senior Partner of a firm of architects and surveyors. Study the traditional cellular office layout for the offices of your firm detailed in Fig 3. Imagine that your company is moving into a modern office block and is to occupy a whole floor which has to accommodate these offices in a landscaped format.

a Reposition the personnel, furniture and equipment. A breakdown list of all staff, furniture and equipment is given below. Use the blank floor plan provided in Fig 4.

   Staff list (total of 30 staff)
   1 Senior Partner
   1 Financial Director
   2 Junior Partners
   6 Architects/Architectural Assistants
   5 Surveyors/Valuers
   2 Clerical Officers
   2 Secretary/Personal Assistants
   1 Typing Services Supervisor
   5 Typists
   2 Reprographics Staff
   1 Mail Room Clerk
   1 Telephonist/Receptionist
   1 Person Friday

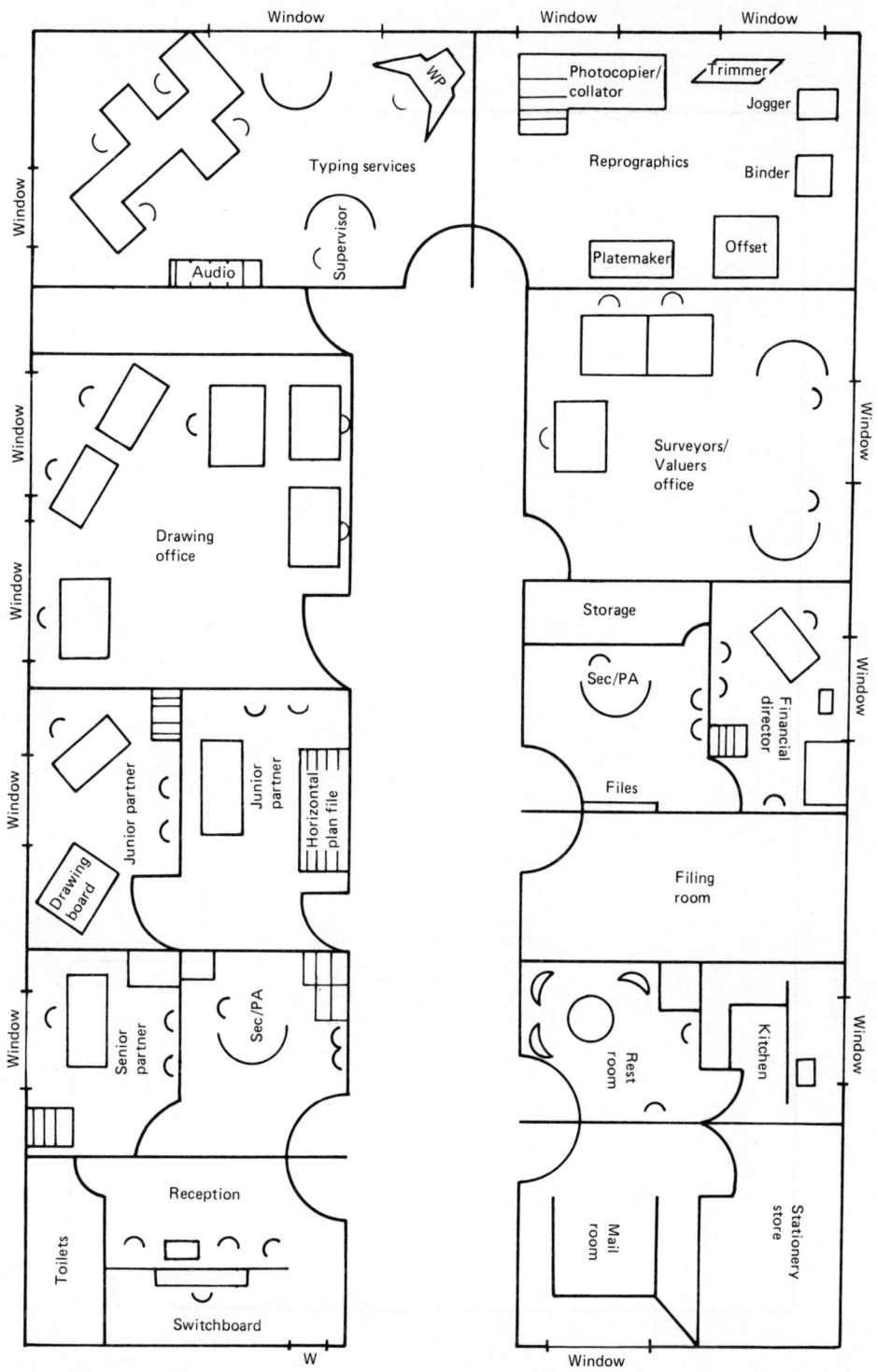

Fig 3

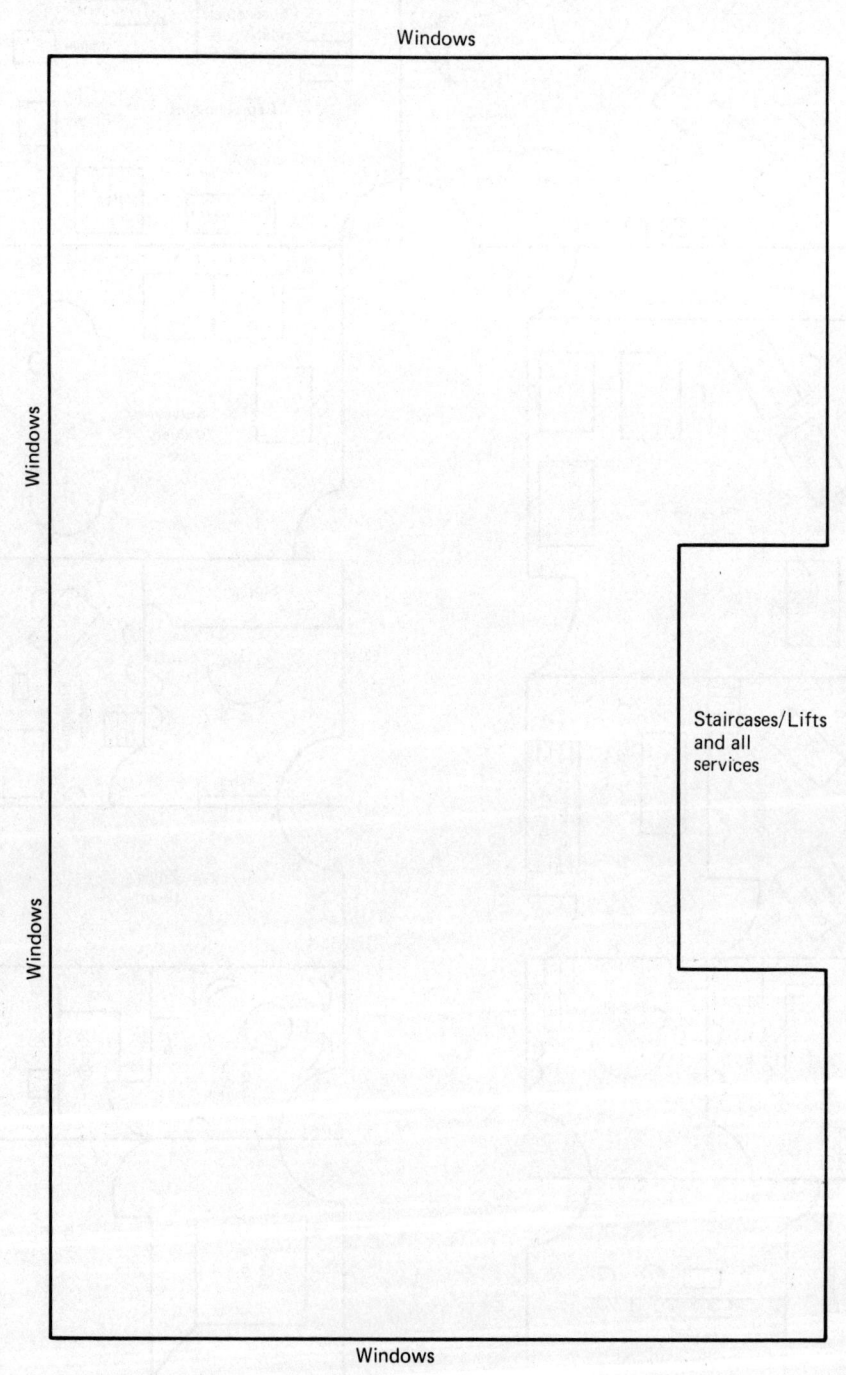

Fig 4

Furniture and equipment
essential desks and chairs for all staff and visitors
7 drawing boards
audiodictation system – bank of machines currently in Typing Services
1 large photocopier/collator
1 platemaker
1 offset machine
1 binder
1 jogger
1 guillotine/trimmer
switchboard
filing/indexing equipment
mailing equipment

b Provide a list of any additional fittings and supplies which you think would be necessary to make the new layout a success. These items should be included and appropriately labelled in your diagram.

Personal activities

1 Take the opportunity to scan through any business/office equipment magazines which are taken by your school/college library or are perhaps even delivered directly to your section. Note the latest developments in office layouts, furniture design and general accessories which are found in modern offices.

2 If you have the chance to visit any offices where friends or relatives may already work, do not pass up the opportunity. It is always interesting to compare workplaces and to begin to formulate your own ideas of what you think makes for good working conditions.

3 Study your local press and Job Centre advertisements to gain an impression of the sorts of office jobs which are currently available. Build up a collection of varied job advertisements from the press and compare and contrast descriptions in terms of qualifications required, the qualities and experience sought and the salaries and conditions offered.
Note: This selection of job advertisements will be required for use in Unit 8.

Group activities

1 Identify any services in your school or college which are centralised, and discuss whether you think the centralisation is an advantage or a disadvantage.

2 What specific functions do you think your school or college office performs?

3 Imagine that you have been given the opportunity to design and equip a new model office for use by students of secretarial procedures at your school or college. What sort of office (size/shape of room(s)) would you like to have, and how would you like to see it set out? If you have an artist in your group, why not draw a plan?

4 How important do you consider job titles to be? What useful purpose do they serve?

5 Collect a selection of job advertisements from your local paper. Discuss what you think the jobs are likely to involve, and what sort of qualifications, qualities and experience the organisations are likely to be looking for.

3 Recruiting and training staff

Aim of the unit

The unit provides information on procedures in the recruitment and selection of office staff and offers guidance in applying for positions in an office. It also considers training methods and the appraisal of office staff.

Specific objectives

At the end of this unit you should be able to:

1 Complete application forms.
2 Write your personal curriculum vitae.
3 Compose letters relating to job applications.
4 Prepare simple job descriptions for positions relating to office work.
5 Draft job advertisements.
6 Outline the personal preparations to be made by you prior to attending an interview.
7 Describe the detailed steps leading up to an appointment.

8 Explain the purposes of an induction programme.
9 Suggest the likely content of an induction course.
10 Compare and contrast different forms of training.
11 Explain what is meant by 'staff appraisal'.
12 State the advantages of merit rating.

Self-testing warm-up

1 Why is it important to select good staff?
2 What are common sources of recruitment for office staff?
3 What are the main points to be included in a job advertisement?
4 What are the important things to remember when completing application forms?
5 What is a curriculum vitae?
6 What is the purpose of an interview?
7 What sort of preparations are likely to have been made by the firm conducting the interview?

8 What is a testimonial?

9 What sort of things should be included in a letter of appointment?

10 Which piece of legislation requires workers to have a written statement of their terms of employment?

11 What is a job description, and what should it include?

12 What is meant by 'induction'?

13 What do you understand by 'on-the-job training'?

14 What is meant by 'appraisal'?

15 What are the advantages of merit rating schemes:

    a to employers

    b to employees?

Situation-based activities

Situation 1

Imagine that you have just read the following advertisement in your evening paper.

Naturana Health Products

require a

Junior Secretary

for their expanding Sales Department based in pleasant offices in the city centre.

Good standard of general education essential, together with appropriate secretarial skills. This post would be ideal for a suitably qualified school or college leaver.

Holiday arrangements honoured. Salary negotiable. LVs.

For further details and an application form contact Miss Hanson, Personnel Department, Lord Street, Anycity.

You send for further details as requested – write a suitable letter – and receive the following information together with an application form

Study the details carefully and complete the blank application form (Fig 5).

Details accompanying the application form
Naturana Health Products is a flourishing company engaged in the preparation and distribution of health foods and associated products. It has four branch offices in the United Kingdom, one in France and one in Germany. Its manufacturing outlet is in the Midlands.

The operation started as a one-man (one-woman actually!) business in the early 1960s and such was its early success that a partnership was soon formed, which was later to develop into a limited liability company. In 1978 the company went public and has been going from strength to strength ever since.

The company is progressive in its thinking and working conditions are excellent.

Job description

Title	Junior Secretary
Department	Sales
Immediate superior	Personal Assistant to the Sales Manager
Responsible to	Sales Manager
Authority over	Two departmental typists, one clerical assistant and one office junior
Job function	To perform such secretarial duties as outlined by the Sales Manager or his Personal Assistant, consistent with the efficient operation of the Sales Department of this branch of the company, and oversee the general support work of junior staff as and when considered necessary
Promotion prospects	Senior secretary within the company secretarial structure
Working hours	A 38-hour week. Flexitime in operation

APPLICATION FOR EMPLOYMENT

Vacancy

SURNAME (block letters)	FORENAMES
	Mr/Mrs/Miss

ADDRESS

Tel no

Age last birthday	Date of birth	Nationality Place of birth	If registered under Disabled Persons (Employment) Act YES/NO

EDUCATION Schools attended	From	To	Examinations passed (state subject, board, level and grade attained)
Colleges, university attended			Qualifications attained
Training courses attended			

Membership of professional or other similar associations

Hobbies/sports/other interests

Fig 5

DETAILS OF PREVIOUS EMPLOYMENT (Please commence by stating your present employment first. Use an additional sheet if required)

Name and address of employer	From	To	Brief description of duties

Earliest date at which you could take up this appointment	Present salary
	£ per annum

Names and addresses of *two* persons to whom reference may be made in relation to your experience and suitability for this post

ADDITIONAL INFORMATION in support of your application. You may continue on a separate sheet if necessary

Signature	Date

Fig 5 (contd)

APPLICATION FOR EMPLOYMENT

Vacancy *RECEPTIONIST*

SURNAME (block letters)	FORENAMES
BRIGGS	~~Mr/Ms~~ Miss JAYNE

ADDRESS 72 DEVONSHIRE CRESENT
SPRING PARK
ANYCITY   AB1 2CD

Tel no 0392 65229

Age last birthday	Date of birth	Nationality BRITISH	If registered under Disabled Persons (Employment) Act ~~YES~~/NO
18	05/03/68	Place of birth BATH	

EDUCATION
Schools attended

	From	To	Examinations passed (state subject, board, level and grade attained)
St. MICHAEL'S SCHOOL	1973	1980	
THE KINGSWAY SCHOOL	1980	1984	GCE 'O' LEVELS: ENGLISH LANG (AEB) A ENGLISH LIT. (AEB) C FRENCH (AEB) B MATHS (AEB) C HISTORY (AEB) B

Colleges, university attended

	From	To	Qualifications attained
SPRING PARK COLLEGE FE	1984	1985	COLLEGE DIPLOMA IN RECEPTION WORK RSA TYPEWRITING STAGE II RSA AUDIO-TYPING STAGE I RSA DIPLOMA IN GENERAL RECEPTION

Training courses attended

Membership of professional or other similar associations

Hobbies/sports/other interests

TENNIS, SWIMMING, READING, SINGING
MEMBER OF LOCAL AMATEUR OPERATIC SOCIETY.

Fig 6

Details of previous employment (Please commence by stating your present employment first. Use an additional sheet if required)			
Name and address of employer	From	To	Brief description of duties

Earliest date at which you could take up this appointment MID AUGUST	Present salary £ —— per annum

Names and addresses of *two* persons to whom reference may be made in relation to your experience and suitability for this post

MR J C MASON HEAD OF DEPT. – BUSINESS + GENERAL STUDIES SPRING PARK COLLEGE OF F.E. FULTON ROAD SPRING PARK, ANYCITY	MR . R.J PARK. JOHNSON + PARK. (OPHTHALMIC OPTICIANS) 99 HIGH STREET ANYCITY

Additional information in support of your application. You may continue on a separate sheet if necessary

I have worked during the past 2 summer vacations in Johnson & Park (ophthalmic opticians) where I undertook general reception duties.

My college course specialised in Reception work and I am anxious to obtain a position in which I can put into practice the skills I have acquired.
I enjoy meeting people and feel I have the personal qualities to make a success of such a position.

Signature   *Jayne Briggs*   Date 2 July 198—

Fig 6 (contd)

Specific duties/responsibilities

1 To receive dictation from the Sales Manager or his Personal Assistant and transcribe accordingly.

2 To attend meetings in the absence of the Personal Assistant.

3 To prepare non-confidential mail for distribution within the department; to ensure that all outgoing mail is ready for dispatch at the end of the day.

4 To maintain an efficient filing system.

5 To receive incoming telephone calls and take messages as necessary.

6 To supervise and check the work of junior staff as necessary.

Situation 2

For this series of tasks assume that you work in the Personnel Department of Naturana Health Products.

a Draft an advertisement for a Receptionist. This advertisement would appear in the local evening paper.

b Prepare a suitable job description for this Receptionist.

c Draft an assessment grid which might be used for shortlisting candidates for the position of Receptionist.

d Fig 6 is the application form of Jayne Briggs, one of the candidates shortlisted for the Receptionist's post. Write to Jayne asking her to attend for interview on an appropriate date two weeks from now.

e Compose a letter to be sent to Jayne's referees.

f Devise a checklist which can be used by you and the Personnel Department in preparing to interview the *six* candidates you have shortlisted.
Note: Each candidate will be expected to undergo a telephone test.

g Devise a suitable assessment form to be used by the interview panel in conducting these interviews.

h Compose a letter offering the position to Jayne Briggs.

i Compose a letter to be sent out to unsuccessful candidates.

j Prepare, using the blank card provided (Fig 7), a personnel record card for Jayne.

k To date, indicate the documents you would expect to find in Jayne's personnel file.

l Devise a suitable induction programme for all new office staff.

Situation 3

Assume that you are once again working for Miller & Dobson PLC referred to in the previous units. As a practising secretary within the company you have been asked to contribute to the induction programme arranged for new office staff. You have been specifically asked to talk about your own job as secretary (select the department of your choice from Fig 1) and about the training you have undertaken since joining the company.

a Prepare notes on the content of your talk under the following headings:

  i the work of my department
  ii where I fit in
  iii details of my work
  iv my personal training programme at the local college of further education and in the company

b Imagine that you are approached shortly after the induction programme by one of the newly appointed secretaries. During the induction session she did not fully understand the merit rating system used in Miller & Dobson and feels worried about it. Explain to her in simple terms, what is involved and what you think is good about such a system.

Personal activities

1 Prepare your own curriculum vitae. Try either to type a very good copy or better still, if you have access to a word processor, to place it on disc.

Surname	Forenames	Date of birth	Nationality	Name change	Sex
Address		Change of address			
Tel no		Tel no			
Education		Dates	Qualifications		
Date interviewed		Nat Insurance no		Record of illness	
Job offered	Job accepted	Bank account no			
Department/section		Union membership			
Occupation		Disablement reg no			
Further training details		Appraisal record		Transfer of employment — Date — Reason	
				Termination of employment — Date — Reason	
Employee number	Surname	Initials	Date of birth	Present post	Grade

Fig 7

2 Compose suitable letters to accompany your CV:

  a for a specific post advertised in your local paper

  b to an organisation of your choice as an unsolicited enquiry

3 Open a job file. You should already be collecting advertisements as recommended in Unit 2. Devise a system of classification for the different advertisements you have collected, eg according to job title, according to qualifications required, according to age range stipulated, according to type of organisation or according to salary – it's up to you to choose! Compare the styles of the advertisements, the requirements specified, the salaries quoted and the modes of application required (application form, letter, CV, telephone). Paste the advertisements on to plain paper, leaving ample space around them for your own comments.

Note: You will need this information to complete tasks in Unit 8.

4 Draft a letter which you might send to a local college of further education requesting information about day release and evening courses which they run for secretarial students.

5 Draft a letter to your employer requesting release from work one hour earlier on a Wednesday afternoon to enable you to attend an evening course in word processing.

Group activities

1 Consider possible sources of recruitment for employers. What are the advantages and disadvantages of the different methods, both from the employer's point of view and from yours as a prospective recruit.

2 How ought one to dress for an interview?

3 What sort of questions might you reasonably expect to be asked at an interview? Why do you think you might be asked such questions?

4 Suggest suitable questions which might be put to candidates for the position of Junior Secretary in Situation 1 and to candidates for the position of Receptionist in Situation 2.

5 What differences, if any, would you expect to find between applicants for the position of Junior Secretary and applicants for the post of Receptionist?

6 To be successful in an interview, what do you consider to be the main points to look out for, and what pitfalls ought you to try to avoid?

7 Discuss the essential ingredients in a good induction scheme and design a suitable induction programme for new office staff.

8 Discuss the sort of additional training you would favour once you are employed, ie on the job or off the job?

9 Discuss your attitudes towards the possibility of having job appraisal once you begin work.

4 Communicating effectively

Aim of the unit

The unit emphasises the importance of effective communications within an organisation and highlights the secretary's role in this vital area.

Specific objectives

At the end of this unit you should be able to:

1 Compose memoranda.
2 Prepare a report.
3 Compile a written message.
4 Write business letters of a general nature.
5 Write a letter of complaint.
6 Reply to a letter of complaint.
7 Design a formal invitation.
8 Reply positively and negatively to formal invitations.
9 Prepare a notice for a notice board.
10 Write an article for a house journal.
11 Draft a press release.
12 Design a telephone message form.
13 Provide notes of guidance on the use of the telephone.
14 Prepare material for a telephone answering machine.
15 Compare and contrast good and bad telephone techniques.
16 Provide details of the range of telephone services available.
17 Provide details of the range of telephone equipment and accessories currently available.
18 Compare and contrast different methods of communication.
19 Choose the best method of communication to use in a given circumstance.
20 Identify the factors which would influence your selection of communication media.
21 Estimate possible future developments in communications.

Self-testing warm-up

1 What are the essential features of effective communication?
2 What features of the secretary's role involve her in communicating?
3 Lots of factors influence choice of media. What are they?
4 What are the advantages and disadvantages of oral communications?
5 What are common methods of communicating orally?
6 What are the advantages and disadvantages of written communications?
7 What are the common methods of written communication?
8 What is an intercom system?
9 How does a bleeper system work?
10 What is telex?
11 What is Datel?
12 What special telephone services do British Telecom provide for subscribers?
13 What are the advantages and disadvantages of telephone answering machines?
14 When might a businessman find facsimile transmission useful?
15 What other communication media are available to businesses?

Situation-based activities

Situation 1

Imagine you are Secretary to Jason Winthrop, the Managing Director of Markland Plastics PLC, a manufacturing company with plants throughout the United Kingdom. You are based at the head office in Southampton. The following are tasks which require your action and attention:

a Mr Winthrop wants you to send out, on his behalf, a memorandum to all departmental heads advising them of the new car parking arrangements which are due to come into effect in two weeks' time. He wishes you to stress that unauthorised parking will lead to problems for the many large lorries which deliver raw materials and collect finished goods from the site. Staff must be instructed to park *only* in the areas indicated on the plan (which you should prepare and attach to the memo). Staff must also display *blue* permits at all times.

The memo should also explain the procedure for visitors. Visitors to the site must report at the gatehouse on arrival. There they will be issued with *yellow* permits and directed to the visitors' car park. Heads of department should instruct their staff to notify the gatehouse, in advance if possible, when they are expecting a visitor.

Materials required
1 A4 memo form which you should design yourself
1 A4 site plan which you should draw from your imagination!

b Draft a report on the effects of the introduction of flexitime within Markland Plastics. Assume that this system has been on trial for two months and that you have been requested to submit a report on how it has been received by staff and whether it ought to be implemented permanently. The report will be submitted for consideration by the management at the next full meeting of the board next month.

Materials required
This task should be submitted on A4 paper – typed if possible.

c Mr Winthrop has asked you to notify Fiona Robinson in the Typing Pool that she has been awarded the David Markland Prize for consistent progress in her studies.

You should also prepare an entry for inclusion in the company house journal.

d Mr Desmond Crawford, Sales Director of Paramount Packaging in Birmingham (tel 021 727 9656) telephoned while Mr Winthrop was out. He would like to receive details of Markland's latest developments in clear plastic self-cling packaging material and to meet Mr Winthrop at the earliest possible opportunity. Your conversation with Mr Crawford led you to believe that Paramount could be a valuable potential customer, so you have tentatively made a luncheon appointment with him when he is in Southampton next Thursday. Will Mr Winthrop please confirm. Compose a suitable message, inventing suitable dates, places and times.

e Write a letter to Information Processes Limited, 29 Duke Street, Southampton complaining that their representative failed to keep an appointment to demonstrate a new record processing application of their microcomputer which you are considering installing in the Personnel Department. Assume that the appointment was confirmed by Information Processes several weeks ago and that you had made all the necessary arrangements at your end to release staff from their duties and to set up a room for the demonstration, as well as booking lunch in the staff restaurant.

f Design an invitation card for the opening of the new sports and social complex attached to Markland Plastics. The opening is to be marked by a cheese and wine party in the foyer of the building in six weeks' time on Thursday from 1930 to 2100. All members are invited to attend and to bring one guest each, and replies are required.

Materials required
Invitation cards should be typed on A6 card.

g Write a suitable article announcing the opening of the sports and social complex for insertion in the local newspaper. The article should be between 200 and 300 words in length. Your copy should be presented – typewritten if possible – in double line spacing.

Situation 2

Imagine you are a secretarial assistant with Trans-Continental Holidays PLC, a travel company in Lincoln. Your duties are extremely varied, but much of your work involves placing and receiving telephone calls. The company has recently taken on a junior assistant and she has been put in your charge. In this role please complete the following tasks:

a Design a telephone message form to be used within the company by all personnel taking mesages.

b Write a letter to Mr and Mrs J Henderson, 22 Saville Crescent, Lincoln confirming their booking of a two-week Italian holiday (one week in Rome, one week in Sorrento) and acknowledge receipt of their £60 deposit – the balance to be paid eight weeks prior to departure. Add any other information which you consider might be helpful and relevant. The holiday reference is RS/BA/7214/JUL.

c Trans-Continental Holidays have just had a telephone answering machine delivered. This is to be used to provide a 24-hour service for customers. This means that it will be set up with a prerecorded message for people calling after office hours, and it will also enable callers to leave their names and numbers and details of their enquiries so that they can be dealt with promptly the next day. Prepare a message to be recorded by you for the machine.

d Prepare a memorandum notifying all staff of the installation of the new telephone answering machine.

e As part of your job you are occasionally asked to attend meetings of local societies and talk about holidays. On this occasion you have been particularly asked to talk about bargain break weekends in England. Prepare a talk which will last about twenty minutes. You should talk about the idea in general and then select two different weekends and provide details on them. You should also prepare a brief handout for distribution at the end of your talk.

f Among your tasks for today you have set aside half an hour to speak to the new office junior on the importance of good telephone technique. What sort of things would you stress, and how would you ensure that she has your uninterrupted attention while you are talking to her?

g Devise a mock telephone exercise which you can try out with the new junior to help assess her present technique and point out any obvious weaknesses she might have. Assume that the telephone equipment you have will enable you to carry out such a test in privacy.

h Prepare a guidance sheet on telephone usage to give to the junior.

Situation 3

Assume that you are Personal Secretary to Mr Geoffrey Firbank, a partner in the solicitors' firm of Briers, Firbank & Taylor in Poole, Dorset. Mr Firbank has many outside interests including the presidency of the local golf club for this year and the chairmanship of the Rotary Club. As well as carrying out your work for the firm, you often oblige Mr Firbank by attending to matters relating to these activities.

The following tasks have to be dealt with by you today:

a Prepare for Mr Firbank's signature a business letter to Mrs Geraldine Hilary of 29 The Grove, Branksome Park, Poole, Dorset BH13 6J6 informing her that the drafting of her will has been completed and is ready for her approval and signature. Suggest a suitable date and time, one afternoon towards the end of the week.

b Reply to a letter of complaint which the firm has received from Mr Delamere of 652 Ringwood Road, Parkstone, Poole BH14 4NA (Fig 8). Mr Firbank's car broke down on a country road on the way back from Wimborne and by the time he managed to telephone the office Mr Delamere had gone. The letter should be suitably apologetic as Mr Firbank did hope to secure Mr Delamere's business!

c Mr Firbank has received the two invitations in Fig 9 (page 34). He has asked you to accept the invitation from Lymington Golf Club to

attend their annual dinner and to send an apology to the Wareham Antiquarian Society. Write suitable replies on his behalf.

Personal activities

1 Try to improve your telephone technique.

2 Read aloud. Listen to your own voice (use a cassette recorder). How do you sound? Could you sound better? Why not try to improve your speech? perhaps you speak too quickly or at a very high or low pitch. These are things you can easily rectify. Don't worry if you feel you have a regional accent. This is perfectly acceptable as long as you speak clearly and distinctly and what you say is grammatically sound.

3 Listen to others – in person, on the telephone, on the radio, on TV. Be critical. How do they come across? What makes one better than another?

4 Read more carefully. Is the material written in a way you can understand first time, or do you have to reread? If it's the latter, why do you have to reread? Were the sentences complicated in their construction, was the writer using words you didn't understand, or was the material badly expressed?

5 Where it is appropriate, always write thank-you letters. They do not take long to write and are always appreciated – often much more than a quick telephone call.

Exercises on telephone technique

Study the following telephone conversations. Compare and contrast them, indicating the principal differences in technique. Be critical in your comments and point out any errors and omissions you notice.

Conversation A

Secretary	Good morning, Mr Robinson's office, his secretary speaking.
Caller	Could I speak to Mr Robinson please?

```
                                      652 Ringwood Road
                                      Parkstone
                                      POOLE
                                        Dorset
                                          BH14 4NA

                                   18 September 19..

    Briers, Firbank & Taylor
    Solicitors
    Lloyds Bank Chambers
    POOLE  Dorset
    BH7 9LT

    For the attention of Mr Geoffrey Firbank

    Dear Mr Firbank

         I very much regret the necessity of having to write this letter
    but feel obliged to remind you that I have a very busy schedule and
    consequently consider it vital that all my appointments are honoured.
    Your failure to keep our appointment of yesterday resulted in my
    wasting the major part of the afternoon when I could very easily have
    spent the time in a constructive way.

         Also I feel that it is amiss of your office not to notify me
    should you be unable to keep an appointment.

         Your firm came highly recommended to me and I am extremely
    disappointed that our first encounter should end in this way. I have
    a lot of very important business for which I require sound legal
    guidance and am anxious to establish a relationship which will be
    fruitful to both parties.

                        Yours sincerely

                        Charles Delamere

                        C Delamere
```

Fig 8

Secretary	I'm sorry, Mr Robinson is out of the office this morning. Can I help you or take a message?
Caller	Well, he and I were chatting the other evening at the squash club about microcomputers, and he suggested that I should have a demonstration of your new one here in our office and that if I could get a suitable date and time organised at my end he would bring a machine along and do the demonstration.
Secretary	I see, and you are?
Caller	Phillips of Winston & Green.
Secretary	Have you settled on a date and time, Mr Phillips?
Caller	Well, yes, as a matter of fact I have. Next Tuesday morning would be perfect if you can manage that?
Secretary	I am looking at Mr Robinson's diary for next week and it does seem alright for that time, but I shall have to confirm it with him. May I call you back later when I have spoken to Mr Robinson?
Caller	Yes, that would be fine.
Secretary	Could I have your telephone number, please, Mr Phillips?

```
        LYMINGTON GOLF CLUB

    requests the pleasure of
 .......GEOFFREY FIRBANK...............

 at their ANNUAL DINNER ·to be held on

 Friday 25 October 19.. at Peasford House
 Hotel, Lymington - 7.30 pm for 8.00 pm.


 RSVP
```

```
 WAREHAM ANTIQUARIAN SOCIETY

   requests the pleasure of
 ....Mr & Mrs. G. Firbank.............

 at a Cheese and Wine Party to be held

 at Major & Mrs Dewhirst's, The Steading,
 Grange Road on Friday 25 October 19..
 at 2000 hours.

 RSVP
```

Fig 9

Caller	Sorry, of course, It's 837 6511 extension 279.
Secretary	Thank you. That's 837 6511, extension 279. I'll call you back later, Mr Phillips, and we can finalise all the details then.
Caller	Thank you very much. Goodbye.
Secretary	Goodbye, Mr Phillips.

Conversation B

Office Junior	Hello.
Caller	Is that the Sales Department?
Office Junior	Yeh.
Caller	Could I speak to Mr Fowler please?
Junior	He's not here. He went out to lunch a couple of hours ago and I haven't seen him since. He should have been back ages ago.
Caller	Could I leave a message for him?
Junior	Yeh, if you like.
Caller	Could you ask him to call David Symonds about the arrangements for next week?
Junior	OK. Hang on a minute, though, till I get a pen. (*Long pause*) Who did you say you were again?
Caller	My name is David Symonds and I would be grateful if he could call me as soon as possible about the arrangements for next week.
Junior	Right oh. Bye. (*Hangs up*)

Now rewrite Conversation B as it ought to have taken place.

Go back to Conversation A and prepare a message for Mr Robinson, assuming that you are his secretary.

Group activities

1 Form groups of four or five to discuss topics of your choice. Why not select something of current interest from the press? Elect a reporter from each group; that person is to make notes and summarise the content of the discussion for the benefit of the other groups at a plenary session to be held at the conclusion of the discussion sessions.

2 Select a topic for debate and have two speakers for and two against. Choose something that has two readily identifiable points of view. The remaining group members vote for and against the topic debated on the basis of the effectiveness of the arguments put forward by the speakers.

3 Form a panel of four for 'Any Questions'. Elect a question master. The remaining members of the group form the audience and put forward the questions for the panel. Questions should be concise but clear and varied in content. The question should be repeated by the question master, who then requests the views of the panel by asking each member to speak. Finally the question master must be prepared to summarise the views at the end of each question.

Note: Wherever possible, video/tape record such session so that they may be played back and criticised constructively afterwards.

5 Applying the secretarial role

Aim of the unit

This unit provides the opportunity to enact the role of a secretary via a series of integrated tasks and assignments which a practising secretary could realistically expect to encounter in her daily routine.

Specific objectives

At the end of this unit you should be able to:

1 Accurately complete a diary.
2 Keep an appointments book.
3 Devise a suitable bring-forward system.
4 Prepare briefing notes for a junior member of staff who will stand in for you in your absence.
5 Indicate how you would deal with a persistent newspaper reporter.
6 Outline the arrangements you would make for an informal buffet luncheon in the committee room of your organisation.
7 Prepare a brief talk to be given to the secretarial students at your local college.
8 Make travel arrangements.
9 Prepare an itinerary.
10 Book hotel accommodation.
11 Identify the priority task from a selected in-tray.
12 Suggest how you would handle a difficult situation in the office.
13 Give advice to a fellow secretary.
14 Indicate how you would attempt to establish a good working relationship with your boss.
15 Indicate the problems you could expect to encounter when taking on the work of an additional executive.

Self-testing warm-up

1 How would you distinguish between a shorthand typist and a secretary?
2 What would be a secretary's likely preparations prior to taking dictation for her boss?

3 Why do discrepancies arise in diary keeping?

4 When making appointments, what are *four* things you should always bear in mind?

5 When receiving visitors on behalf of your employer, what should you remember?

6 How would you deal with a sales representative who has not got an appointment?

7 What sort of *aide-mémoires* might a competent secretary use?

8 Apart from travel, what sort of arrangements might a secretary make?

9 When making foreign travel arrangements, what points must be clarified in advance?

10 Why is maintaining confidentiality an important aspect of a secretary's role?

11 How can a secretary help maintain confidentiality in her daily routine?

12 What do you think are important aspects in a secretary's relationship with junior staff?

13 Why is it becoming increasingly common for a secretary to work for more than one executive?

14 What sort of things make for a secretary's poor management of her time?

15 When an organisation is about to appoint secretarial staff, what sort of additional qualities are they likely to look for in applicants?

Situation-based activities

Situation 1

You work for Jonathan Taylor, the Sales Manager of a large wholesale builders' merchants in Leeds. Mr Taylor has worked with the company for over forty years, having progressed from a minor position as a school leaver to his current post. He is due to retire in two months' time and is anxious to call on all his old customers and generally leave things organised for his successor. This means that he will be out of the office a lot as customers come from quite a few distant locations. Business is extremely good at present and the general work of the office has to be kept going. Mr Taylor's successor has still to be appointed.

a Study Mr Taylor's diary for next week and decide which evening would be best for him to have dinner with a business colleague in Scarborough. He would stay overnight. Please book him into a four-star hotel and supply the details. Plan his return route to Leeds to take in a call to York, where we would like you to book a table for four for luncheon at a convenient hotel. Use suitable reference books to provide the information you require.

DIARY
APRIL

Monday 21	Thursday 24
0930 Progress Meeting	
1230 Lunch - Metropole Hotel - TJ	1400 — Interview Panel
1530 Mr Spencer - Hargreaves & Co	
Tuesday 22	**Friday 25**
1000 University - Works Dept	1000 Bradford City Council
11.30 Phil Jackson - Fairbrothers with MD	1430 Works Council Meeting
Wednesday 23	**Saturday 26**
1500 - Bill Giles, Personnel re next weeks interviews (15 mins only)	
NOTES	**Sunday 27**

b It has come to your notice that the staff are planning a very elaborate farewell for Mr Taylor, and you know that he would prefer something less ostentatious as he has talked with you about it quite often. How will you attempt to influence this situation to the satisfaction of everyone?

Also you have been asked to try to find out what sort of farewell gift Mr Taylor would like. How would you try to do this?

c Today, whilst Mr Taylor is out of the office, a sales representative with whom he has had frequent dealing in the past has arrived without an appointment. How would you deal with this?

d You have received an invitation to address a group of secretarial students at the local college of further education on secretarial work and the sort of qualifications, skills and qualities which employers are looking for. Prepare notes for your talk.

Situation 2

Imagine that you work as Secretary/PA to a Member of Parliament. Conditions are somewhat cramped in the House of Commons and you share an office with another MP's Secretary, Sylvia, who is much less experienced than you. Several problems have arisen over the past few weeks and you need to resolve them as quickly as possible. How would you handle them – tactfully, as you like Sylvia as a person and know you will have to continue to work together.

a Sylvia is extremely untidy, and her papers are continually spilling over into your work area.

b When you have been out of the office and Sylvia has answered your telephone, she has often left an insufficient message; you have had the problem of attempting to interpret it on your return, by which time she may not be there to clarify.

c Yesterday when you came back from lunch a friend of Sylvia's was seated at your desk reading an internal memo that was directed to your MP.

d Sylvia frequently interrupts your work with queries about hers.

e Sylvia is always discussing her MP's work with you over coffee and lunch breaks and enjoys endulging in the general gossip and rumours which circulate in a place like the House.

Situation 3

You work in the Housing Department of a local authority and your immediate superior is Mr Jones, the Housing Manager.

a When you get to the office this morning at 0845 the following items/tasks/messages are in your in-tray. Explain how you would deal with each one and state the one to which you would give priority, giving reasons for your selection.

   i minutes from last week's meeting of the Social Services Committee on which Mr Jones sits

   ii a letter addressed to Mr Jones and marked 'Personal'

   iii a note from Mr Dickson from Environmental Health saying that he cannot keep the luncheon appointment he has with Mr Jones today

   iv a note written by Mr Jones to you last evening at 1930 asking you to check that an overhead projector is in the committee room for the meeting which he is scheduled to chair at 0930 hours

   v a message from the switchboard taken at 0835 hours to say that Mr Jones will not be in the office till after 1000 hours as his mother has been taken ill suddenly and he has gone to the hospital

   vi this month's copy of the local authority calendar of events

   vii apologies for absence from Robert Mayer for this morning's meeting

   viii the copy of a monthly journal which Mr Jones always circulates to his assistants in the first instance

b Much of the work of the Housing Department is centred around the outcomes of meetings and much of the correspondence received cannot be dealt with until after such meetings.

Explain the sort of bring-forward system you might devise, and how you would deal with the correspondence in the mean time.

c Prepare notes of guidance for a junior member of staff who will stand in for you whilst you are on holiday:

   i in preparing correspondence for signature
   ii in making appointments
   iii in taking dictation
   iv in maintaining confidentiality

Situation 4

You work for a busy public relations firm in the centre of London. Life is extremely hectic and you need to coordinate the daily activities of three executives.

a What sort of problems are you likely to encounter?
b What sort of diary(ies) would you keep for them?
c Give *ten* 'pearls of wisdom' on the effective management of time to a new secretary who has just joined the company and is working for two executives for the first time.
d Outline the arrangements you would make to organise an informal buffet luncheon in the committee room for two days' time.
e Knowing that you work for a public relations firm, a girl friend who is also a secretary has asked your advice about getting on with her boss. She has just gone to a new job and feels that her new boss is constantly comparing her, sometimes unfavourably, with his previous secretary who has just retired. What advice would you give her?

f Your company is involved in the launch of a new product which is attracting a lot of interest in the media. You have had three persisent telephone calls from a reporter already this week and now he has arrived in your office. What will you do?

Situation 5

You are required to undertake the travel arrangements for three of the staff within your organisation. One is going to the USA on a three-week coast-to-coast lecture tour. The second is visiting two of the organisation's subsidiary companies – one in Lyons, the other in Barcelona – and is travelling by car, as his wife is going to join him later in Spain for a two-week holiday. The third is attending a four-day sales convention at Gleneagles Hotel in Scotland, where he is scheduled to give a presentation on the third day of the company's latest promotional item.

Describe the preparations and arrangements you would make on behalf of each, clearly indicating the unique aspects of each trip and the reference books and other sources you would use to help you.

State the special items (eg passports, tickets, maps) each will require, and how you will arrange to contact each in his absence.

Situation 6

You work for Mr Reginald Lamont, the Export Manager of an electronics company which has substantial commitments overseas, particularly in Europe. Mr Lamont is the President of the Staff Association within the company. From the assorted information given below, enter the material as it would appear (a) in your executive's diary and (b) in your own diary for the month of February. Design suitable diary layouts for this activity.

14 February	Staff Association Valentine's Day Dance – 8 pm Sports Centre
22 February	Mr L is due to travel to Brussels on business. He will stay for three nights at the Europa Hotel and will fly British Airways as usual. He needs currency organised.
8 February	Mr L's daughter's 21st birthday. You are invited to her party on the following Saturday at the Lamont's home (6.30 pm)
3 February	R & D Committee Meeting – committee room 1430
5 February	lunch with Neville Mariner of Lexitron Fibres – 1230 Britannia Hotel, Carlton Room
19 February	tentative arrangement to see Herr Winckl from Hamburg
21 February	finalise agenda for Export Directors' Meeting in one week's time.

Personal activities

1 Keep *two* diaries, one for personal use (appointments, birthdays and special events), the other for school/college events (homework, examination dates, meetings, term dates).

2 When you go on holiday with your family or friends, devise a travel itinerary and prepare a countdown calendar as you near the departure date. Take a particular interest in all the travel arrangements and necessary bookings as well as insurance cover and the arrangements for currency.

3 Be prepared to volunteer to help with the organisation of any social event the family is arranging. Much of the organisation is the same as for major business events!

Generally try to be more organised in your daily life.

Group activities

1 Discuss the advantages and disadvantages of working for more than one person.

2 Choose some sort of informal event which you and your fellow students might like to arrange and consider the organisation involved. Prepare a checklist and assess how much time it would take to arrange such an event. Examples might be:

a a buffet luncheon
b a visit to the theatre
c a day trip to some place of interest

3 Imagine that you have to organise a four-day visit to Paris for people in your class.

a List the steps you would take.
b Devise an interesting itinerary.
c Prepare a checklist for those going.

4 From your knowledge of a secretary's role and function and from reading the press, discuss why secretaries may be security risks. What steps can be taken to minimise this:

a by companies
b by individual secretaries

5 Discuss how you might make more effective use of your work and leisure time.

Role play

Devise a role play exercise where you are the secretary and one of the group is:

a your boss
b another secretary with a problem
c a junior member of staff
d an important visitor
e a visitor without an appointment
f a client with a complaint
g a representative from a firm of office equipment suppliers
h the manager from a firm of outside caterers
i a travel agent
j the Company Chairman

6 Preparing filing and indexing systems

Aim of the unit

The unit emphasises the importance of efficient record management and provides the essential foundations for devising appropriate filing and indexing systems.

Specific objectives

At the end of this unit you should be able to:

1 Define filing.
2 Suggest reasons for inefficient filing.
3 Identify the essential ingredients of a good system.
4 Set up an appropriate system from a given set of circumstances.
5 Compare and contrast different methods of classification.
6 State the advantages and disadvantages of different methods of classification.
7 Provide simple rules for filing.
8 Explain cross-referencing.
9 Select appropriate filing equipment.
10 Explain the operation of a Central Filing Department.
11 State the advantages and disadvantages of central filing.
12 Select suitable filing accessories.
13 Set up and maintain an indexing system.
14 Compare and contrast various indexing methods.
15 Explain the need for a retention policy.
16 Describe possible uses of microphotography.
17 State the advantages and disadvantages of microfilm.
18 Suggest ways of storing microfilm/fiche.
19 Indicate the points to be borne in mind when selecting equipment.
20 Devise suitable systems for personal use.

Self-testing warm-up

1 Why is filing important to an organisation?
2 What are the reasons for filing?

3 What is the basis of most filing classifications?

4 What could be meant by the 'word system' in connection with filing?

5 What is a tracer?

6 What is meant by 'signalling'?

7 What sort of numerical classification system is often adopted by large organisations?

8 When would a geographical classification be useful?

9 What are the drawbacks of geographical filing?

10 What factors would you bear in mind when selecting a method of classification?

11 What advice would you give to a junior who is filing for the first time?

12 What do you understand by the term 'archival storage'?

13 What sort of documents have statutory requirements for the length of time they are filed?

14 Why might an organisation consider microphotography?

15 What do you understand by the term 'COM'?

Situation-based activities

Situation 1

You work for a firm of chartered accountants in a medium-sized country town. There are four partners in the firm, and in total there are just over 200 clients ranging from large limited companies in the agricultural market to small sole traders. The firm also handles the calculation of wages for five farms in outlying districts as well as taking on personal taxation queries for private individuals. A senior member of the clerical staff has just retired and you have been given the responsibility of maintaining accurate records for the firm.

a Imagine that you spend the first few days familiarising yourself with existing systems. What sort of systems would you expect to find in operation? Give examples.

b Suppose that one of the partners has asked you to consider ways of improving the system in terms of:

  i the space utilised

  ii the speed with which documents can be retrieved

  What suggestions might you make?

  In addition, £500 is made available to you to spend on equipment and supplies. How would you consider spending this sum in order to gain maximum benefit?

c Assume that you are given *carte blanche* to alter the existing system and that you can make major changes which will obviously affect the staff who use the files. What steps would you take to ensure that all staff are aware of the changes and that the new system can come into operation with the minimum of disruption.

Situation 2

Assume that you have just moved job from a small company with departmental filing and taken up a position as Secretary within a large organisation with a full-scale Central Filing Department.

a What are the main differences you are likely to encounter?

b What are the advantages and disadvantages likely to be?

Situation 3

Your organisation is moving to new premises in the city centre. The new offices are largely open plan in design and the public has ready access to the office area. At present records are kept in a variety of locations; a range of different systems are used, and the equipment and methods are far from standardised. It is important that the company presents a well-organized image to its clientele, and new multipurpose equipment is envisaged.

a What sort of equipment might be considered?

b In what ways could the company attempt to standardise?

c What factors must be borne in mind in selecting new systems and equipment?

Situation 4

Assume that you work within the Central Filing Section of a large hospital and that you are responsible for instructing new junior staff in the operation of the system and the importance of total accuracy and the maintenance of strict confidentiality. Prepare notes for yourself, together with suitable illustrative examples to help you explain the procedures to three new junior filing clerks with no previous experience.

Situation 5

Imagine that you have just been appointed Secretary/PA to the Managing Director of a new company and that at present very few files exist. The work of the company is internationally based and very technical in nature, and covers four main areas of interest. Some of the documentation will have a legal nature and much will be confidential.

The company is expected to expand rapidly in the next few months. Your boss is a stickler for detail and expects efficiency in record management and follow-up procedures.

a What sort of systems would you set up initially?

b What equipment and materials would you require?

c Which systems of classification would you select for different aspects of the work, and why?

d What follow-up techniques might you initiate?

e How would you attempt to ensure strict confidentiality in your systems?

Situation 6

Your company is about to have its records transferred on to microfilm/fiche. Identify any

problems which might arise and state what preparatory steps would require to be taken to facilitate the transition.

Also, describe the sort of equipment that the company will need initially to become operational in the minimum time, and the additional equipment that might be required/considered in due course.

Situation 7

Your boss is constantly complaining that files are being removed from the cabinets without any indication of their whereabouts. This can result in lengthy delays and considerable inconvenience. He asks you to devise a system to improve matters. What would you do, and how would you attempt to ensure that staff adhere to your system?

Personal activities

Filing and indexing is an area of secretarial work which you as a student can put into practice every day. You will have many things you could and possibly should file, so why not devise your own systems?

Examples of things you might file will include:

a your school/college notes for all your different subjects

b press cuttings you collect

c records and cassettes

d personal bills/receipts, bank statements

In a personal system you have the freedom to exercise any sort of method you like. It can be as simple or as complex as you care to make it, and you can incorporate all sorts of cross-referencing techniques, codes, follow-up systems and guides as you would find useful.

What sort of systems might you find it convenient to set up? Ask yourself these questions:

1 What do I need to file?

2 How do I keep things at the moment?

3 Is it efficient? Can I always find things when I want them?

4 If not, why not?

5 How many different categories of information do I need to file?

6 How do I think of them or refer to them?

7 Which sort of order makes best sense?

8 Do I need everything with me all the time?

9 What can I do to make things stand out?

10 At what point, if any, can I discard things?

11 Will the system I have in mind cost much?

12 Would a separate index prove useful?

Answering these few simple questions in relation to your personal record management should help indicate the possibilities open to you in relation to setting up your own filing/indexing system(s).

Group activities

Practical filing and indexing

Rearranging lists of names, topics, places, numbers or whatever on paper is all very well, but is no substitute for physically handling cards, papers and folders. Filing and indexing is to some extent like shuffling cards – one becomes better with practice. Sometimes it is not very easy to gain realistic filing practice in the classroom, but the following activity can prove a worthwhile preparation in providing the sort of materials which you can usefully use later to practise your actual filing skills.

What will you need?
a a telephone directory
b an atlas or AA/RAC book
c an examining board's syllabus
d the birthdays of your classmates
e blank cards (ideally coloured), or if unavailable, coloured sheets of paper

This is what you do
If using cards, maximise the space by drawing them up as in Fig 10.

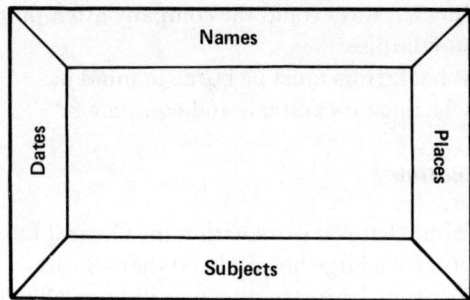

Fig 10

1 At random select as many names as you like – say twenty per set of cards – and write or type them neatly in the same space on each card.

2 Using an atlas or AA/RAC book select place names – again at random – and complete the cards accordingly.

3 Similarly, complete the areas with subjects and dates.

4 You should now have several sets of cards of sheets with four categories of information recorded.

5 Shuffle the cards or papers and make sure that you have the categories all the same way up.

You now have the basis for a practical filing activity.

Using a stopwatch, time one another in sorting the cards/papers into correct filing order.

It will be useful to devise solutions to check the accuracy of your filing. To save still more time you can code all your names/dates/places/subjects, and then you simply need to call out the codes for checking purposes.

Another practical suggestion

Where you are fortunate enough to have a model/training office in which you undertake practical activities, it should be possible for you to devise and set up filing and indexing systems for all manner of things. The following are some examples:

1 File personal files, colour coded for all different classes. These could be prepared alphabetically, or a personal number could be allocated to each student making use of the facilities. (Where the latter method is selected, it will, of course, be necessary to prepare a separate index.)
2 File all past examination papers.
3 File all handout materials.
4 File all practice exercises and solutions.
5 File all details on equipment and supplies.
6 File back copies of magazines and periodicals and cross-reference accordingly.
7 File all audio material used in practical activity sessions.
8 File all blank forms, headed paper and materials.

These suggestions should provide you with some initial ideas and you should be able to utilise a wide range of equipment and a variety of systems of classification.

7 Using office systems and procedures

Aim of the unit

The unit emphasises the need for sound systems and procedures within an organisation and provides practice in using and designing commonly found procedures.

Specific objectives

At the end of this unit you should be able to:

1 Devise a simple procedure for issuing office stationery.
2 Devise a system for keeping accurate stock records.
3 Design an appropriate form for the requisition of stationery.
4 Keep an accurate petty cash book.
5 Calculate flexitime.
6 Identify the features of a good form.
7 Design an expenses claim form.
8 Design a form requesting leave of absence.
9 Design a form for recovery of telephone charges for personal calls.
10 Design a form for requesting reprographic services.
11 Issue a set of instructions to all personnel regarding the procedure to be followed in dealing with visitors to the premises.
12 Prepare a report on the investigation into procedural problems in the Mailing Department.
13 Outline the main provisions of the Health and Safety at Work Act 1974.
14 Devise a safety checklist for use in an office.
15 Prepare notes of guidance for office workers on safety.

Self-testing warm-up

1 What is meant by a system or procedure?
2 Why do organisations need systems?
3 What makes for a good system?

4 Why is it important to have a procedure for handling mail?

5 Why should all members of staff be familiar with the procedure for dealing with mail?

6 What sort of equipment will be likely to form part of a procedure for handling outgoing mail?

7 Why is it necessary to have a system of stock control?

8 What is meant by petty cash?

9 How does the imprest system work?

10 How does flexitime work?

11 What are the advantages of flexitime to both staff and management?

12 Why is it necessary to control the use of forms within an organisation?

13 What factors have to be considered in designing forms?

14 What office procedures tend to utilise forms?

15 What are the principal duties of employees in respect of health and safety at work?

16 What are the underlying reasons for accidents of any kind?

17 What are the most common causes of office accidents?

Situation-based activities

Situation 1

Imagine that your boss has asked you to be responsible for the issue of stationery within your department, as the present system (or lack of one!) is resulting in chaos. Staff are helping themselves from the stationery store, and when they have used up supplies items are frequently out of stock for long periods; there is also a high level of wastage. Eventually the intention is that this duty should be delegated to a more junior member of staff, but you have been given authority to get a new system organised and running smoothly in the first instance.

a Explain, in detail, the steps you would take to reorganise the stationery store.

b How would you determine what stock should be carried?

c How would you record the stock?

d Design a form for staff to requisition supplies.

e Outline the procedure you have devised in a memo to all staff.

Situation 2

Imagine that one of your duties is the maintenance of the petty cash for your office. You work in a firm of solicitors. You are given a monthly sum of £30 to use in this connection. From the vouchers shown in Fig 11 overleaf, complete a suitable petty cash book with appropriate analysis columns and balance it at the end of the month, ready for checking by the Chief Accountant. The month in question is June. Take into account the following additional details:

a a receipt for £4.50 for a bar lunch which one of the accounting assistants was asked to take with a representative

b a receipt for 68p for biscuits which the Office Junior bought on the Senior Partner's instructions

c £1.70 in cash which was given to you by a client for a long-distance telephone call made from your office

Situation 3

Your organisation has started a scheme of flexitime based on the daily splits given in Fig 12 (page 49). The following apply:

a In any week you must work a minimum of thirty-five hours.

b The accounting period for flexitime is four weeks.

c The maximum working day is nine hours on Monday to Thursday, and eight hours on Friday.

d The maximum carry-forwards at end of an accounting period are plus ten hours and minus seven hours.

e Flexileave is one day or two half-days per accounting period.

You plan to have a long weekend during the

Petty Cash Voucher   Folio 1   Date 3 June

For what required	Amount £	p
Bus fares	2	40
	2	40

Signature *g Wild*
Passed by *V P Jones*

Petty Cash Voucher   Folio 2   Date 6 June

For what required	Amount £	p
Recorded delivery packet	–	52
	–	52

Signature *Susan Bryden*
Passed by *V P Jones*

Petty Cash Voucher   Folio 3   Date 11 June

For what required	Amount £	p
Train fare	7	75
	7	75

Signature *Tom Williams*
Passed by *H Peters*

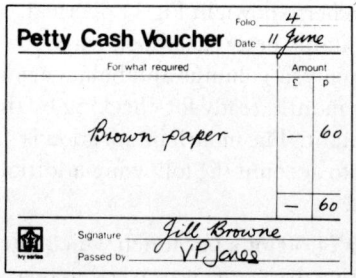

Petty Cash Voucher   Folio 4   Date 11 June

For what required	Amount £	p
Brown paper	–	60
	–	60

Signature *Jill Browne*
Passed by *V P Jones*

Petty Cash Voucher   Folio 5   Date 12 June

For what required	Amount £	p
Window cleaning	1	50
	1	50

Signature
Passed by *H Peters*

Petty Cash Voucher   Folio 6   Date 15 June

For what required	Amount £	p
Registered letter	1	20
	1	20

Signature *Susan Bryden*
Passed by *V P Jones*

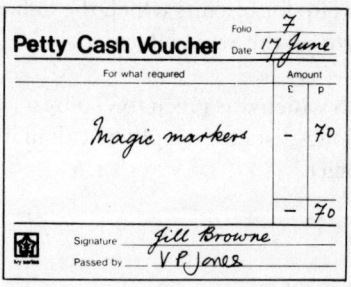
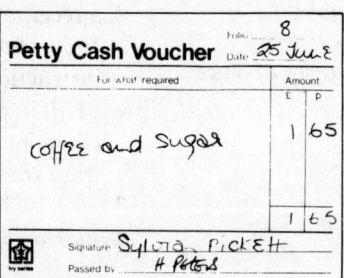

Petty Cash Voucher   Folio 7   Date 17 June

For what required	Amount £	p
Magic markers	–	70
	–	70

Signature *Jill Browne*
Passed by *V P Jones*

Petty Cash Voucher   Folio 8   Date 25 June

For what required	Amount £	p
Coffee and sugar	1	65
	1	65

Signature *Sylvia Pickett*
Passed by *H Peters*

Petty Cash Voucher   Folio 9   Date 25 June

For what required	Amount £	p
Milk bill	–	80
	–	80

Signature
Passed by *H Peters*

Petty Cash Voucher   Folio 10   Date 26 June

For what required	Amount £	p
Flowers for Reception	1	75
	1	75

Signature
Passed by *H Peters*

Fig 11

Monday-Thursday

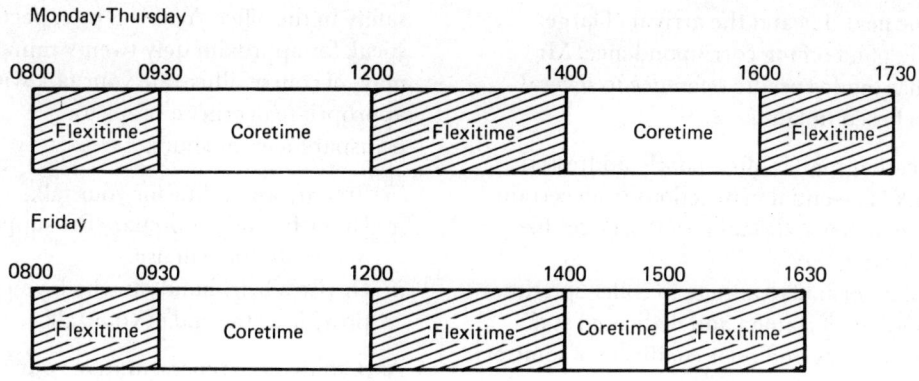

Fig 12

next accounting period. You hope to leave at midday on the Friday and return to work at 1400 the following Monday. You also hope to visit the hairdresser in a two-hour lunch break on the Thursday before the weekend.

To achieve your minimum of thirty-five hours per week you usually work the set hours 0830–1230 and 1330–1630 each week, ie seven hours per day.

a On the week prior to the weekend in question, how much time do you have to make up to ensure you work thirty-five hours, and how might you arrange this?
b On the week following the weekend, how much time do you have to compensate for the hours lost on the Monday morning, and how might you do this?

Situation 4

You are working in the Forms Control Section and you are asked to design suitable forms to standardise the following procedures throughout the organisation:

a claiming expenses
b requesting leave of absence
c recovering telephone charges for personal calls
d requesting reprographic services

Design four suitable forms.

Situation 5

You work in an organisation where the monitoring of visitors is important at all times. In recent weeks strangers have been found attempting to park their vehicles in the company car park, and also wandering about inside the building. This constitutes an obvious breach of security. In fact, in most instances they had appointments with your personnel but no proper arrangements had been made to ensure that their arrival was expected, that the relevant department or individual was notified of the arrival and that the visitor knew where to go.

You have been asked to prepare and issue a set of instructions which have to be followed by all personnel in relation to the standard procedures which should be taken when visitors are invited on to the premises.

Draw up a suitable set of instructions:

a for visitors travelling by car
b for visitors arriving on foot or by taxi or public transport

Situation 6

You work for Mr Forsythe, the Personnel Manager of a large company. He has been receiving a series of complaints from Mr Wilkes, the Senior Mail Clerk, about the late arrival of mail to the Mail Room and the consequent need for staff to work late in order to clear this mail before the next day and the arrival of large quantities of incoming correspondence. Mr Wilkes has made specific reference to several points in his complaints:

a the fact that mail is often poorly addressed

b the lack of essential instructions from certain offices which use special postal services like recorded delivery

c the failure of staff to adhere to collection times

d his shortage of trained and dedicated staff

e the inadequacy and poor condition of some of the equipment.

Mr Forsythe has asked you to investigate these complaints over the next two weeks and to report your findings and recommendations to him in the form of a report which he will use as the basis of his submission when the problem is considered at the next meeting of the Management Committee. (For this activity you will need to use your imagination. The five points raised by Mr Wilkes provide you with a starting-point, but do not hesitate to suggest other reasons for the problems and to elaborate on the five already given.)

Situation 7

You are the Typing Pool representative on your organisation's Safety Committee, which meets once a month to report on any problems relating to health and safety at work and generally to discuss ways of stimulating and improving safety awareness within the company.

There is a substantial recruitment campaign currently in progress and this will bring about the employment of new members of staff, many of whom will not have worked before and consequently will be unfamiliar with the requirements of the Health and Safety at Work Act 1974.

a The Chairman of the Safety Committee – the Company Safety Officer – has approached you with the request that you contribute to the safety induction programme planned for new staff. He would like you to concentrate on safety in the office. You will be expected to speak for approximately twenty minutes and may, of course, illustrate your talk with appropriate overhead projector transparencies or slides.

  i Prepare an outline for your talk.

  ii Describe and/or prepare the supporting materials you will use.

  iii Devise a brief handout which you will provide at the end of your talk.

b As Typing Pool representative your supervisor has asked you to help her draw up a code of practice which all Typing Pool personnel should adhere to in an attempt to maximise safe working habits. In addition she considers that you should prepare a safety checklist which the Technician should use on a monthly basis to check the electrical equipment in use in the section.

  i Prepare your suggestions for inclusion in the code of practice.

  ii Draw up a suitable checklist for the Technician.

c At the next meeting of the Safety Committee, two of the items on the agenda are as follows:

Ideas for a forthcoming safety campaign within the company
A visit from the Safety Inspectorate

As a conscientious committee member you wish to make a worthwhile contribution to the meeting.

  i Suggest two ideas which might be incorporated into the safety campaign.

  ii Indicate the sort of preparations which your section will make prior to the visit of the Inspectorate.

Personal activities

The nature of this unit is such that the most valuable thing you can do on a personal basis will be to use any contacts you may have with people who already work in a business or office and see if they can supply you with any of the following:

1 Copies of safety policies and instructions from their organisations.
2 An opportunity to study any staff handbook material which may be issued to them in respect of procedures to be adopted.
3 Specimen blank forms for systems and procedures in operation within their organisation.

It will be interesting to study and compare the different documents you manage to gather with a view to assessing their effectiveness.

Ultimately you could pool resources with other members of your group or class and see just how many different types of forms the group is able to come up with, how they compare and in what ways they are noticeably different.

Group activities

The following are suggestions for activities you might choose to undertake as a group, both in practical workshop-based lessons and in a more rigid classroom situation as topics for discussion.

1 Devise and prepare a range of suitable forms for use within your model or practice office.
2 Where necessary, draw up sets of instructions which should be followed by those using training office facilities. Examples of essential instructions could be as follows:

   a instructions for borrowing reference books
   b instructions for the issue of materials, ie the updating of a stock control system
   c instructions for operating equipment, eg the photocopier

3 Devise a rota system for using different items of equipment within your training office or workshop.
4 When people talk about systems and procedures they often tend to associate them only with forms and form-filling. How realistic a viewpoint do you think this is? Discuss.
5 Study and discuss the following statements:

   Sound systems and procedures generally lead to easier and more efficient working.
   All form-filling is a boring activity and is only necessary for bureaucratic reasons.
   Adherence to strict systems and procedures takes all the flexibility and spontaneity out of work.

6 Do you think working on flexitime would be good, and would it be an added attraction if offered in a job advertisement?

8   Working with business facts and figures

Aim of the unit

The unit examines the principal areas concerned with business facts and figures – their role in business operations, the documentation, and their calculation and presentation – which will be applicable to a secretary and which she can expect to meet in the course of her work.

Specific objectives

At the end of this unit you should be able to:

1 Trace the documentation involved in the completion of a business transaction.
2 Identify and explain the purpose of basic business documents.
3 Distinguish between cash and trade discounts.
4 Identify the various services offered by commercial banks.
5 Compare and contrast a standing order with a direct debit.
6 Explain the operation of the credit transfer system.
7 Differentiate between a loan and a bank overdraft.
8 Differentiate between a cheque card and a credit card.
9 Explain the advantages and disadvantages of credit cards.
10 Prepare a bank reconciliation statement.
11 Briefly explain the process for the calculation and making up of wages.
12 Suggest alternative means of remuneration for employees.
13 Analyse a salary slip.
14 Explain the functions of the principal income tax forms.
15 Identify different ways of presenting data.
16 State the advantages and disadvantages of visual presentation of data.
17 Prepare different forms of charts and graphs.
18 Devise simple flow charts.

19 Design overhead projector transparencies.
20 Establish possible uses for visual planning/control boards.

Self-testing warm-up

1 In what ways might an organisation receive enquiries?
2 What information is contained on an invoice?
3 Where an organisation adopts multiple-copy invoices, where might the additional copies go?
4 When might a company send out a debit note?
5 It is not strictly essential in every circumstance to send a receipt when payment is received; why not?
6 Suggest *six* services which a current account customer of a bank may use.
7 Name *two* types of bank account other than a current account which you might choose to operate.
8 Other than the *six* mentioned above, suggest *four* services which banks provide for their customers.
9 Give an example of one occasion when you might use (*a*) a standing order and (*b*) a direct debit.
10 When would a bank overdraft be preferable to a personal loan, and why?
11 Identify two ways in which wages might be calculated.
12 What does MIRAS stand for?
13 Provide *five* things which National Insurance covers.
14 What is a P45?
15 When do employees receive a P60, and what does it show?
16 How might you differentiate between the lines in a multiline graph?
17 What is a histogram, and when might you use one?
18 What is the principal disadvantage of a pictogram?
19 Give *two* examples of situations where it would be appropriate to construct a model.

20 What are the advantages and disadvantages of visual planning and control boards?

Situation-based activities

Situation 1

You work for a manufacturing company in the Training Section. It is customary for all newly appointed school/college leavers who join the staff of the company to spend several weeks in each department. In so doing they gain an appreciation of the overall work of the company as well as form an impression of the area in which they might most like to work once their training period is complete.

As with any manufacturing organisation, the paper work necessary to complete a business transaction is considerable, as is the movement of paper between different departments during the completion. In one of your training sessions your boss, the Training Officer, always gives a talk on the document cycle involved in the completion of a business transaction from the initial enquiry to the receipt of payment by the customer. This can be difficult to grasp, and he would like you to help him prepare suitable materials to support his talk.

a Devise a flow chart identifying the business documents involved and trace the transaction from start to finish. This chart should be capable of transfer to overhead projector (OHP).
b Suggest any other supporting slides/OHPs which might be prepared and used to good effect.
c Prepare a brief handout describing the following principal documents:

catalogue/price list	invoice
order	debit note
advice note	credit note
delivery note	statement

Situation 2

You work in the Personnel Department of your company and have just been approached by a newly appointed junior member of staff with the following questions:

a Why have I been asked to open a bank account?
b What do I need to do, and where should I open it?
c Which sort of account should I open?
d Will I get one of these cards for getting money from the wall?
e How does the system work from the point of view of the firm?
f How will I know where I am with my money?

What will you tell her, and what extra advice might you offer?

Situation 3

You have had a bank account for several years now and have just received a form through the post for you to complete in order to receive a credit card. You did not ask for this form to be sent to you, and are now debating in your own mind whether you ought to complete it. You already have a cheque book and cheque card. To help you decide what to do, list the points for and against having a credit card.

Situation 4

Your employer is soon to travel to Italy on important company business. He will be in Rome and Naples for between eight and twelve days and will be travelling extensively during that time. He wants to be sure that he will always have sufficient funds to meet all expenses incurred. However, he has had money stolen on a previous business trip and is somewhat apprehensive, knowing the colourful reputation which Italy has for pickpockets.

Also, he is hoping to pull off a big business deal on behalf of the company and will need substantial funds to ensure that he can secure the business on the spot.

a What advice would you give in relation to the

day-to-day money matters involved? Give full details in support of your suggestions.
b How can he arrange for acceptable financial backing to support any business deal he may be successful in setting up?
c How would you secure additional advice on both these matters, and what sort of questions would you need to ask?

Situation 5

During your coffee break this morning you got into conversation with someone from the sales force of your company. He was talking about a friend of his who works for a rival firm, and how that firm pays their sales representatives on a strict commission basis, in contrast to your company which operates a flat rate plus commission. Your office junior was also at the coffee table, and afterwards asks you to explain what he was talking about as she didn't understand a word of it.

Explain in simple terms, and also tell her about the bonus and incentive schemes operated by your organisation.

Situation 6

Assume that you work for a company which pays its salaried staff on a monthly basis directly into their bank accounts so that all that is received by staff on 'pay day' is a salary slip.

A new member of staff, Josie Walls, has just joined your section and is receiving a salary for the first time in her working career (she has previously worked only on a part-time basis and was always paid in cash). When she opens her first salary slip (Fig 13) she asks you to go through it with her and explain what each item means.

Situation 7

A relative of yours has recently set up in business for himself. Knowing that you work in an accounts department, he has asked your advice on the difference between his first bank

Fig 13

Dept	Employee No	Employee name	NI number	NIC type	Tax code	Tax year	Tax month	Month ending	Annual salary
05	0297	WALLS J	TP 24 1900D	D	0 200L	1985/86	03	30.06.85	4525.00

PAY AND ALLOWANCES

Overtime hours	Overtime pay	Basic pay	NI benefit adjustment	Code	Amount	Code	Amount	Code	Amount	Code	Amount	Code	Amount	Gross pay
		434.00												434.00

Deductions (R=refund)

Superann	Income tax	NIC	Union sub Code	Amount	Code	Amount	Code	Amount	Code	Amount	Code	Amount	Total deductions
23.24	89.70	24.30	79	3.00	56	1.00							141.24

TOTALS TO DATE IN THIS EMPLOYMENT

Pay less superann	Tax deducted	NI deducted	Superann. (Net pay scheme)	Stat. sick pay	Net pay
410.76	89.70	24.30	23.24		292.76

PREVIOUS EMPLOYMENT

Pay	Tax deducted

Examples of codes:

Allowances

01	Car allowance
02	Laundry allowance
03	Rent allowance
04	Travel expenses
05	Materials allowance

Deductions

52	Court orders
53	Housing rent
54	Hospital contributions
55	SAYE
56	Charity

statement, which he has just received, and what he thought his account held. At present there is £230.55 less in the bank than he had envisaged.

a Explain the factors which can contribute to this difference by providing suitable examples.
b Provide a specimen bank reconciliation statement, using very simple figures, to illustrate your explanation still further. Commence with the balance as indicated in a bank statement, and work back to that shown in an individual's own cash book records.
c Repeat this exercise, but this time start from the cash book and work towards the bank statement figures.

Situation 8

Assume that you act as Secretary to Mark Richmond, the Sales Director for an international company. A lot of your work involves statistical presentations and calculations. It is the annual sales convention in four weeks' time, and Mark has to present a report which will require the preparation of appropriate charts and graphs to suitably illustrate a lot of complex statistics.

He gives you the following three sets of information, and asks you to prepare suitable diagrammatical presentations which he can use in conjunction with an overhead projector whilst submitting his report to the convention.

a Figures to enable him to show a comparison of the total sales both at home and abroad for the past six years:

	Home	Abroad
5 years' ago	150 000	50 000
4 years' ago	250 000	150 000
3 years' ago	350 000	250 000
2 years' ago	300 000	200 000
Last year	450 000	300 000
This year	600 000	450 000

b Total product sales (at home and abroad) of the six major items which the company produces, expressed as total unit sales provided to the nearest 5000 units:

Product	Total units	Export units
A	75 000	30 000
B	50 000	20 000
C	65 000	45 000
D	30 000	10 000
E	55 000	20 000
F	40 000	10 000

Note from Mark: I'm not sure whether these would be better presented as a composite bar or as two separate ones. Could you try both and we'll decide later? Thanks meantime.
c The proportion of sales on different products this year:

Product	Proportion
A	3/8
B	1/16
C	1/4
D	1/8
E	1/16
F	1/8

Situation 9

Imagine that you work for a development corporation. In three months' time it is due to open its next major project – a shopping precinct designed to meet the needs of a recently occupied housing estate.

a Your superior, the Project Manager, likes to plot progress towards such deadlines. Devise a suitable chart which will enable him to indicate the ideal schedule for the three final major activities involved, namely painting and decorating, shop fitting and car park layout. The painting and decorating is scheduled for completion at the end of week 8; the shop fitting midway through week 10; and the car park midway through week 11 of the twelve-week period leading up to the official opening. Your chart should be easy to follow.

You will need to use your imagination and creativity.

Once you have completed the initial task, assume that you have reached week 5 and for the purposes of comparison indicate *clearly* the actual progress made (once again, use your imagination!)

b In the countdown for the official opening you are likely to be involved in the preparation of other forms of diagrammatical/visual back-up material which will be used in the following forthcoming instances:

  i General publicity material
  ii Advance press coverage There has to be a press conference one week prior to opening. This will be attended by representatives of both local and national press. As well as having a conducted tour, they will be given the opportunity to return to the office block to ask questions of the architectural and planning team about the general design and layout.
  iii TV coverage
  iv Magazine coverage Following the opening there will be a full feature in the *Architects' Journal* tracing the development of the project and illustrating it appropriately.

Under each heading indicate the sort of materials you would expect to have to organise and/or assist to produce and prepare, giving reasons for your choice of aid(s) in each instance.

Situation 10

Assume that you work for a research and development team. The executives you work for tend to favour the extensive use of visual planning and control boards for all aspects of the work of the section, including things like product development and the results of market research surveys, as well as general administrative matters like holiday rotas and meeting schedules.

You are due to move into new offices. The existing boards were badly damaged when the decorators tried to take them down from the walls in the old offices. As top priority, three new boards have been ordered together with all the necessary symbols and lettering so that you can replace them. Your tasks are as follows:

a Set up a completely new board to represent the current progress of three products being developed at present. The board should show – *at a glance* – the progress of internal phase tests 1, 2 and 3, packaging trials and external tests, and the estimated commencement date for full-scale production.
b Devise a control board to represent the results of market research carried out on two products in three regions of the country.
c Draw up a four-month planner featuring June, July, August and September. Indicate clearly on the planner the holiday periods of the eight members of staff working in the section, each of whom is due to take up to a maximum of three weeks' holiday over this period.

Personal activities

There is a considerable choice for improving your personal performance with figures and general factual information of a business nature.

For example, take banking as a typical business activity. You need only walk into any branch in your local high street and you are faced with a selection of useful material in the form of information booklets which provide up-to-date details on the numerous services available to both individual customers and businesses. Banks also display boards giving details of interest rates for savers, investors and borrowers, and the larger branches usually display details of the foreign exchange rates operating that day.

Where you have your own account, always be sure to check your statements carefully. Errors do happen and it is in your interests to check for accuracy. Also, checking enables you to gain a clearer picture of the operation of your account.

As mentioned in *Secretarial Procedures*, it is advisable to gather current literature on all matters which are subject to amendment because of either changes in legislation or fluctuations in the bank rate. Therefore, leaflets available from your local post office, the Department of Health and Social Security, building societies, insurance companies and the Inland Revenue can provide useful background information for your studies.

Give thought to your own spending and that of your family. You may even find it interesting to select a commodity (eg newspapers or milk) and plot the expenditure over a predetermined period. When you go to the supermarket, take a pocket calculator and total up your purchases as you go round.

When you are in a restaurant or cafe, check the bill. Note the charge for VAT, and see whether a service charge has been included or whether you should calculate an appropriate tip.

If you use a credit card, consider how best to maximise the credit facility it provides. Also calculate the interest you can expect to pay if you pay only the minimum amount requested on the statement. Interest rates are very high when considered on an annual basis!

Analyse your expenditure over a given period. How do you spend your money? Where might you save? Generally try to be more systematic over money matters. If you intend, for instance, to save money for a holiday, study the alternatives open to you, eg a deposit account, a building society share account, National Savings Certificates, Premium Bonds or perhaps even a 'flutter' on the stock market.

Specific task

Using the job advertisement data you started to collect in Unit 2, provide a statistical breakdown under the following headings:

- salary
- qualifications
- type of experience stipulated
- age range

- type of organisation – function and size
- any other frequently occurring information

You will obviously require a substantial number of advertisements (50 or 100) to make this exercise worth while, informative and interesting. If you have not gathered that many, why not pool resources with others in your group and undertake the activity together?

Group activities

For this unit, the tasks you can usefully do in groups will often take the form of collecting different literature (eg information from different banks) and making a structured comparison of the terms and services offered.

Similarly, where you have time to follow something through over a number of weeks, you can plot progress in the form of charts and graphs. The following are some things you might like to look into:

a exchange rates of say four currencies in relation to sterling
b some shares and their progress
c best-selling books – fiction, non-fiction and paperback – as quoted weekly in the press
d popularity ratings of TV programmes
e the top twenty record charts
f popularity of video films
g your own accurate typing speed (if you type)
h fluctuating petrol prices

Suggested activities associated with your secretarial course

1 Study the hours allocated to the different subjects on your course over a week. Draw up a pie chart which will clearly demonstrate the breakdown of time spent on each subject.
2 Where you have a training office and the opportunity to gain practical experience in the use of a variety of machinery and equipment, it may be possible for you to prepare a visual control board to monitor your progress and that of your group. Simply

list your names along one axis and the items of equipment along the other. Select symbols to represent the degrees of proficiency achieved; eg a circle might indicate satisfactory ability, a square might indicate the need for more practice, whilst a star might signify excellence!

3 Similarly, you can devise a planning board if your course operates on the basis of assignments or phase tests of some kind. Here you can plot those completed, those in the process of completion and those yet to be attempted.

9 Arranging and servicing meetings

Aim of the unit

The unit sets out the purposes of holding meetings, defines the different types, identifies the personnel involved, details their duties and responsibilities, outlines the arrangements required in organising meetings, and explains the underlying procedures and the documentation and terminology involved.

Specific objectives

At the end of this unit you should be able to:

1 Provide reasons for holding meetings.
2 State the advantages and disadvantages of this means of communication.
3 Identify different types of meeting.
4 Distinguish between formal and informal meetings.
5 Explain the duties and responsibilities of the chairman and secretary.
6 Compare and contrast the duties of a committee secretary with those of a minute secretary.
7 Recognise the essential ingredients of effective chairmanship.
8 Define meeting terminology.
9 Explain the essential preparations in arranging meetings.
10 Draw up agendas and notices.
11 Compile suitable minutes.
12 Identify the characteristics of a successful meeting.

Self-testing warm-up

1 State *four* differences between formal and informal meetings.
2 Name *three* types of committee.
3 Provide *four* possible reasons for calling a meeting.
4 What is meant by a 'quorum'?
5 Identify and explain *three* types of agenda.

6 Provide *four* acceptable means of giving notice of a meeting.

7 What constitutes a valid meeting?

8 Give *six* duties of a secretary prior to a regular meeting.

9 Give *three* duties of a secretary during a meeting.

10 Give *three* duties of a secretary after a meeting.

11 Provide *four* qualities which would be sought in a chairman.

12 When might a chairman exercise a casting vote?

13 What is meant by the term 'rider'?

14 In a limited company, which document stipulates the rules governing the conduct of meetings?

15 What is a 'proxy'?

16 What is meant by 'ex officio'?

17 Identify *two* types of minute which might be taken.

18 How should minutes be recorded?

19 What would you look for in a good set of minutes?

20 As a secretary to a committee, what sort of follow-up action might you be required to take?

Situation-based activities

Situation 1

Assume that you are Secretary to Simon Williams, who chairs the monthly meeting of the Finance Committee within your organisation. This is a standing committee of eleven representatives plus Mr Williams, and you have a regular booking of the board room for the first Tuesday of every month at 1400 hours.

In connection with these meetings, you are required to undertake the following tasks:

a Prepare a checklist of all the necessary duties and arrangements you will have to undertake between now (the day after this month's meeting) and the actual day of the meeting next month.

b Prepare a suitable notice and agenda for next month's meeting to be circulated to all committee members. Type this, or use a word processor if possible.

Agendas for these meetings take on a very consistent format, commencing with the three items usual for most agendas and concluding with the usual two items. Next month's meeting has also to discuss a proposed reduction of 3 per cent in revenue allocation to individual departments, the financing of research studies on the part of staff, and the attempt to secure EEC funding in respect of a proposed extension to plant.

c In two months' time you will be on holiday, and Janette, a junior secretary in your department, is going to stand in for you at the Finance Committee meeting. This will be the first time she has acted as a secretary in this capacity, and she has never taken minutes before.

Provide her with some useful advice on both aspects in the form of notes of guidance to which she can easily refer.

Situation 2

Imagine that you are involved in a local action group which is concerned at the possibility of a Motorway development near your village.

You wish to call a public protest meeting to which the press will be invited and you hope to attract substantial interest. How would you publicise this event, and how would the arrangements for this type of meeting differ from those which a secretary would make within a business organisation? Identify specific individuals who, as members of the community affected, might wish to cooperate or take a leading role, and indicate the sort of results you would anticipate from such a meeting, together with the sort of follow-up you would envisage.

Situation 3

Your boss is chairman of the Staff Association within your company. The meeting of the

Association, the main point of which is to finalise details for the annual staff dinner and dance, is scheduled for tomorrow. He has received unexpected instructions to visit head office tomorrow, and it is too late to reschedule the meeting. Unfortunately the vice-chairman is on holiday, so the chairman has asked you to stand in for him (the constitution permits such a substitution!)

What steps would you take to prepare yourself for this meeting, and what points would you try to remember in terms of providing effective chairmanship, bearing in mind that these meetings are relatively informal and that time is always in short supply?

Situation 4

Imagine that a representative from a European subsidiary of your company is spending two weeks in your department as part of an exchange programme. His English is pretty good, but he has just sat in on a very lengthy formal meeting as an observer and is perplexed by some of the terminology he has heard and some of the practices he has observed. He asks you to explain.

a From the following list, provide written examples (rather than pure definitions) of the usage of the terms, so that he will have something to refer to later in support of the verbal explanations you will offer:

quorum	*nem con*
motion	rider
point of order	articles of association
status quo	*ad hoc*
through the chair	on the table

b He also asks you to explain why the chairman had to sign the minute book *twice* and why it appeared to be typewritten as to his knowledge minutes were always handwritten.

Situation 5

The following is the notice of meeting and agenda for the AGM of your local drama society.

Use your imagination and your knowledge of meeting procedure to prepare a suitably annotated chairman's agenda and a set of minutes. The nomination form and the list of productions are given as Figs 14 and 15.

Oakland Drama Society

Notice is hereby given that the Annual Meeting of the Oakland Drama Society will be held in the Rehearsal Room of the Little Theatre on Tuesday 8 May 198– at 1930 hours.

Nominations for office bearers (duly seconded) should be made in writing on the enclosed form and forwarded to the Secretary no later than three days before the meeting. Members are also asked to study the attached list of possible productions for next season as put forward by the present committee. Voting will take place at the AGM for the four productions favoured by the membership

Honorary Secretary

Agenda

1 Chairman's welcome
2 Apologies for absence
3 Minutes of the previous AGM
4 Matters arising from the minutes
5 Secretary's report
6 Treasurer's report
7 Election of office bearers:

   Vice-chairman
   Secretary
   Treasury

8 Appointment of two new committee members to replace those retiring on rotation
9 Reappointment of the Auditors
10 Theatre renovation fund
11 Next season's productions
12 Any other business
13 Date of next meeting

Situation 6

You work in a large manufacturing organisation (select your own commodity preference). A new

```
Oakland Drama Society

Nomination slip

Position.................................................

Name of person proposed...............................

Signature of proposer.................................

Signature of seconder.................................

Date of nomination....................................
```

Fig 14

```
Suggested productions for next season

  1  Ring Round the Moon                Jean Anouilh

  2  Shadow of a Gunman                 Sean O'Casey

  3  Cat on a Hot Tin Roof              Tennessee Williams

  4  Roots                              Arnold Wesker

  5  Who's Afraid of Virginia Woolf?    Edward Albee

  6  The Importance of Being Earnest    Oscar Wilde

  7  In Camera                          Jean-Paul Sartre

  8  The Ghost Train                    Arnold Ridley
```

Fig 15

product is going to be launched in six months'
time, and this will involve a major contribution
from many departments within the
organisation.

Initially, departmental meetings are to be
held prior to a decision by the main executive
committee on the collective information
presented by all departments. In the first
instance meetings are intended to assess the
main implications for the individual
departments arising out of the proposed launch,
and it is envisaged that about three meetings
will be required on a departmental basis.

a Identify the major departments likely to be
involved in the organisation you have
selected.

b Illustrate their involvement in the decision-
making process by means of a diagram.
c Indicate any *ad hoc* committees which might
be set up to facilitate discussions and ultimate
recommendations.
d Adopt a department, and prepare a report on
the assessments reached by your department
as a result of the meetings for presentation to
the executive committee.

The following are suggestions of manufacturing
companies you may wish to consider in reaching
your selection:

- a motor car company
- a company producing breakfast cereals
- a textile company

- a computer software company
- a cosmetics company

Personal activities

1 Collect specimen notices of any public meetings from your local press and try to match these with any reports which follow.
2 Try to obtain copies of company reports from anyone who may have a shareholding in a public company. The formal notice of the AGM, together with the agenda, is usually contained within the document. Proxy cards are also normally included.
3 If you are a member of an organisation or society, attend any meetings to which you are entitled, and gather any documentation which is circulated.
4 Pay particular attention to any meetings – formal or informal – which may form part of a TV programme. Many programmes can offer valuable insight into something of which you may currently have little or no personal experience.
5 Consider attending one of the open meetings of your local authority (council meetings).

Group activities

Meetings form the perfect vehicle to put theory into practice and to exercise your role play skills.

Dependent upon the size of your class, form suitable groups and enact all the stages of meeting preparation, conduct and follow-up. Obvious principal roles will be taken by a chairman and secretary, but it is simple to add predetermined committee figures with particular roles to play.

You can hold mock meetings where you can decide on any topic you like. You can also prepare a suitable notice and agenda together with any other supporting literature to brief the members scheduled to attend the meeting, and one or more of the group can practise taking minutes.

Some practical suggestions

1 It will be interesting if several of you take minutes; write them *all* up and circulate them *all* afterwards. Will you be able to believe that you have all reported the same event?!
2 Why not arrange this activity around a special topic of interest, eg the introduction of office technology, and invite a guest to give a 'presentation' as part of the meeting? This way you will need to organise the following:

a a subject of interest
b a suitable date, time and place
c a possible guest speaker. This will involve an invitation, possibly a briefing discussion in advance, arrangements for the person's arrival (directions, parking, someone to meet him), someone to make a formal introduction and someone to propose a vote of thanks
d any necessary visual aids, eg an overhead projector
e refreshments
f follow-up procedures – minutes, report of the presentation, formal letter of thanks to the speaker

Obviously this can be a demanding but worthwhile and enjoyable exercise provided you have the time available and the necessary facilities at your disposal.

3 As an alternative to a formal business meeting, why not adopt more of a debating format? Choose say three topics; the following are some possible suggestions:

Women in management
Qualifications versus experience
Does technology dehumanise the workplace?
It is better to support your own country's economy than to holiday abroad
The case for and against zoos
Would a Freedom of Information Act be a curse or a blessing?

(Always select topics which have an argument for and against).

Then appoint three chairpersons, three sets of

speakers (two for and two against each motion) and a teller to record votes.

Follow the conventional rules of debate (akin to those adopted in any formal meeting) and apply a strict time allowance. On each occasion the chairperson is required to accept three questions from members of the audience (who should also be making notes of the proceedings), and in conclusion should sum up the case for and against the issue under debate and put the motion to the vote. At this time the teller should count the votes and then pass a paper to the chairperson, who will announce the result.

10   Finding and utilising information

Aim of the unit

The unit provides insight into the wide range of sources available to secretaries for securing and applying information essential and appropriate to their role and function.

Specific objectives

At the end of this unit you should be able to:

1 Indicate sources of information which practising secretaries may call upon in the course of their work.
2 Identify appropriate information resources for given circumstances.
3 Suggest suitable reference books to which a secretary might refer.
4 Recognise the value of good library usage.
5 Consult a library index.
6 Indicate the criteria to be used in selecting any information resource.
7 Construct your own card index information retrieval system.
8 Identify specialist agencies available for securing information.
9 Recognise the need to consult specialists/experts.
10 Compare and contrast information recorded in different newspapers.
11 Use a dictionary more efficiently.
12 Extract information from a telephone directory at greater speed.
13 Explain the uses to which a secretary might put data banks.
14 Provide advice to junior office personnel on the effective use of newspapers and magazines.

Self-testing warm-up

1 Name *five* resources for information which a secretary might use.
2 Indicate *five* criteria which will be likely to

influence the selection of an information resource.

3 Name *four* general reference books you would expect to find in an average office.

4 Name *three* reference books associated with *people*.

5 Name *three* reference books associated with *professions*.

6 Name *three* reference books associated with *travel*.

7 Name *three* reference books associated with the supply of *statistical information*.

8 State *six* items of information to be found in *Whitaker's Almanac*.

9 Provide *four* reasons why a secretary should read a good quality daily paper.

10 When might a secretary use the services of a specialist agency?

11 What is the difference between a general and a technical library?

12 What is the popular name for the classified telephone directory in Britain?

13 What is the difference between a dictionary and a thesaurus?

14 What technological innovations might a secretary call upon by way of an information resource?

15 What do you understand by the term 'human resource'?

16 State *three* personal resources which a secretary might usefully establish to improve the efficiency of her reference to information on a day-to-day basis.

17 Describe briefly what you understand by the term 'data bank'.

18 What is the principal criteria for information to be worthwhile?

Situation-based activities

Situation 1

Assume that you have been newly appointed as a secretary to a busy executive within a medium-sized organisation (the nature of the company's business is for you to select, as is the function of the executive within the company) This is the first secretarial appointment within the particular department, so there are no reference books in the office.

Select *six* books which you would request initially, providing reason for your selection.

Situation 2

Assume that you work for an oil company. This is a highly competitive area of business; such is its significance to the world economy, and so surrounded is it by political controversy, that it frequently features in the news. In your reading of daily newspapers what should you try to do to keep in touch with current events

a for your own benefit

b for that of your immediate superior?

Situation 3

Imagine that you work as a secretary for an author of historical novels. Grammar must be accurate, and it is also essential to research information on people and places to provide authenticity to the stories. This is an extremely interesting but time-consuming activity.

a What reference books would you find directly useful to you?

b What specialist sources and expert opinions would you be likely to consult?

c What sort of system might you devise to record the information you unearth with a view to being able to refer to it in later novels where appropriate?

Situation 4

Your boss is about to spend four days in London. During that time he will attend two business meetings in different parts of the city; one of these will be a business lunch with a client whose business your company wishes to secure, and will have to be at a restaurant of your boss's own choosing. He is also scheduled to visit an exhibition at Olympia, see a play, meet an Italian business associate who speaks no English, and attend a charity concert at the Barbican. Your boss is an American who has only recently come to Britain and he is very unfamiliar with London, having only visited once (as a tourist) several years ago. Also, he has to meet the Italian associate at Heathrow Airport and he does not know what he looks like! All in all it is going to prove a very hectic and somewhat stressful few days, and he is depending upon you to smooth things as far as possible.

You are required to prepare his itinerary for him. What sources of reference would you consult, and what would be your criteria for their selection?

Also, what additional things might you do, and what additional information might you see that he is furnished with in order to ease the four days?

Situation 5

Assume that you work as a secretary for a firm of computer specialists in the Company Secretary's Department.

a What reference books might you find useful:

   i in your work generally
   ii in terms of the specialist nature of the department's work?

b What newspapers and periodicals would you expect to be provided in the company's reception area for the use of visitors, and in the rest room for the information and relaxation of staff.

Situation 6

Imagine that you have been shortlisted for a secretary's job in a local newspaper office. Part of the work is concerned with local community issues and with regional information. Together with the details you received about the interview arrangements, it is indicated that you will be asked to demonstrate your knowledge and awareness of recent issues in the district, eg unemployment, vocational education and training schemes and transport problems.

How would you prepare yourself for the interview, ie what or whom would you consult?

Assuming that you are successful in acquiring the job, what sort of information systems might you establish to speedily retrieve information:

a previously used in newspaper articles
b gathered but not used to date.

Situation 7

Your office junior always expresses amazement at the way in which you are required to scan the newspapers and many journals on behalf of your boss, who is extremely busy and does not have sufficient time to do so himself. Explain to her how you go about this activity, and what sort of material you 'flag' for his attention.

Also suggest to her why she ought to be more methodical in her own approach to the newspapers rather than scanning the popular press for the gossip columns, the stars and the evening's television programmes, taking in little else!

Personal activities

If you really think about it, you find and utilise information every day in life. For example:

- you consult bus/train timetables
- you use radio and television papers to establish what programmes are on and when
- you listen to or watch weather forecasts
- you consider menus in restaurants
- you study your school/college timetable
- you read newspapers and magazines
- you read textbooks
- you look up dictionaries and telephone directories
- you enter and retrieve information from your diary

to name but a few.

What is important is how effectively you use information and how well you make it work for you. Also, how quick are you? Like anything else, practice makes perfection. If you are hesitant about consulting a dictionary you will never make good use of one. To use any reference book efficiently and effectively you must become familiar with the contents and how they are set out. Always study the notes on how to use the book – even a telephone directory has them! In addition, reference books tend to favour their own abbreviations and symbols and it is necessary to study these first of all.

Reference books are designed for *reference*, not for reading from cover to cover. You need to be aware of the ones which will usefully fit particular circumstances you may find yourself in, and to familiarise yourself with their contents and presentation in order that you may dip into them effectively and find what you seek in the minimum time. No one will expect you to memorise the entire contents. Moreover, reference works are constantly changing and most are updated at least annually (hence they are usually very expensive to buy), so there is little point in becoming an expert on *Whitaker's Almanac* for a particular year. Where, on the other hand, you need to refer to information on a regular basis, eg train times, telephone numbers, certain statistical information, conversion tables for weights and measures, temperatures and so on, you will be well advised to devise your own information retrieval system. This may be in the form of a card index, or perhaps a looseleaf book with laminated sheets, suitably 'flagged' as with indexing systems in filing (see Unit 6).

Using the media as an information resource

The following activities are suggested as simple, easily applied examples of ways in which you can make the media work for you, whilst providing you with useful practice in the process of selecting what is worth while and of interest.

1 Acquire *two* daily newspapers of the same date – one a popular tabloid, the other a more serious broadsheet.

   a Select an item of news covered by both and compare and contrast the coverage in terms of factual information, political bias and general content.

   b Turn to the editorial column. Précis one of the items featured as if you were doing so for your boss.

   c Turn to the classified section. Compare and contrast the contents and calculate the respective charges for inserting an advertisement of your own choosing.

2 Study *two* magazines representative of a particular form of business activity eg *Office Equipment* and *Business Equipment Digest*, both of which specialise in office machinery and equipment.

   Objectively compare and contrast the content and layout for one particular month. Decide which one you would favour given the choice, stating the reasons for your preference.

   Note: You can adapt this activity to any other subject area where competitive publications are produced.

3 Preview future programmes on radio and television and select an item(s) of interest and relevance to your course of study. As a home exercise, listen to or watch the selected programme(s) with a view to discussion in the following lesson. If your school/college has the facilities, the programme may be taped for playback during actual lesson time.

Using the library as a resource

As mentioned in Part I of this book, libraries form a vital resource for information and it is in your best interests to cultivate their use. Many people are reluctant to use libraries in that they consider them unwelcoming and even hostile environments. This is to a large extent understandable in that walking into many imposing library buildings and finding one's way around the shelves can be a foreboding prospect, and students are often hesitant at approaching library staff for assistance. What you must always remember, however, is that they are the *experts* and are there to help you. In fact, one of the attractions of their job is to be presented with a challenge in the form of a problem to solve, and that problem/query might well be yours!

Using a library is not knowledge we are born with but knowledge we acquire, and we should never be afraid to seek guidance. Libraries will vary greatly in terms of the books they carry and the services they provide. Your local library will obviously differ from that in your school or college, which will in turn differ again from a polytechnic or university library or one of the huge reference libraries to be found in the major cities.

Finding your way around general textbooks
Searching for reference material is a very different matter from selecting a novel. The books on your subject matter will all be located together, and you should find out the appropriate number reference according to the system of classification and cataloguing adopted by the particular library. You should also find the precise location on the shelves. These two simple steps can often save you valuable time.

Sometimes you will know a book by its title and the name of the author. In that case you can readily establish whether the library carries the text by consulting the appropriate index – in this case the author index. On other occasions you may not have a title or author in mind, merely a topic or subject area, in which case you would consult the subject index in the first instance. Both indexes are arranged in strict alphabetical order and in many libraries today will be available on microfiche rather than on traditional cards.

Using the reference section
An enormous selection of information is quickly and readily available from the reference section in a library. This will include information from dictionaries, encyclopaedias and yearbooks to specialist directories, abstracts and indexes. Familiarity with the scope and nature of the reference section in your own library will repay you time and time again.

It should be noted that many libraries will carry a special 'reference-only' copy of books which are frequently in demand, so even if the shelf copies are already out on loan you may be able to consult the reference copy in the library.

Newspapers, magazines and journals
Just as the reference section provides a variety of useful texts, so too will the journals section, which is likely to carry a wide range of journals and magazines as well as national and local newspapers. Not only are current copies carried but often back copies, sometimes dating back for many years. Examples of journals useful for you will possibly include *Memo, Office Skills, Management Today, The New Statesman, Business Equipment Digest* and so on. Should your library fail to carry a particular journal which you would like to consult, it will be worth mentioning it to the librarian who may well be prepared to add it to the list.

Audiovisual resources
Many libraries are currently establishing video libraries; they already have extensive audio libraries with both cassettes and records to suit all tastes.

Group activities

Many of the activities you can usefully undertake in groups for the purposes of improving your knowledge and skill in handling reference materials and obtaining information will be dependent upon your ingenuity and the enjoyment you derive from a sense of competiton.

For example, if you can form groups and devise questions from the reference books you may have in your training office you will derive much more meaning from them and a bit of fun besides. It is important to mention here that useful practice may be gained using out-of-date books, provided the format remains unaltered and the book is still published! Often your school or college library will be happy to pass on last year's editions for use in your training office or workshop. When you devise questions it will always be necessary to provide suitable keys to check the answers later.

You can also put certain aspects of using reference books to the test for speed of retrieval. For example, where several copies of a dictionary are available you can test the speed with which the meaning of a word can be found. The same can be applied to the use of telephone directories; one person selects a name and challenges the others to find it as quickly as possible. A stopwatch can add to the interest of this sort of activity. It is surprising how big a range there will be between the first and the last to locate the information.

Resources in your own area

Another interesting and useful activity which you can pursue in groups and which will bring you into contact with outside sources is to compile a comprehensive list of resources in the form of specialist/expert agencies in your own town or city. For example, how many travel agents are there and where are they located? Where is the local chamber of commerce, and what services does it provide? How many libraries are there, and are there any specialist ones amongst them? What are the opening hours? Where is the Citizens' Advice Bureau? Which departments of the local authority are open to the public for reference purposes? Does the local newspaper office have its own archives?

Does the local museum carry specialised information on matters of local interest?

If you live in a large city like London there will, of course, be many more specialist agencies such as foreign trade delegations, the offices of government departments, embassies and so on. A survey would certainly prove to be interesting and informative.

Set up your own resource

As has been suggested previously in this book you can, either on an individual basis or in groups, gather much valuable information to support your secretarial studies course. You are living in a rapidly changing world, and the offices of today and tomorrow will certainly be influenced by advances in technology. Textbooks are hard pressed to keep pace with the changes taking place, and you can certainly make a substantial contribution to your knowledge and understanding of office technology and the developments in areas like communications by establishing your own databank of information gleaned from newspapers, magazines and advertising literature. This can be carefully catalogued and made available to all students who utilise the specialist facilities in your school or college. How you choose to set up such a resource will depend on the facilities at your disposal. They may be anything from a range of lever arch or box files, through a card index or visual display boards, to a microcomputer with data base management software into which you may enter all the information you collect for later retrieval and easy updating.

Whatever the method, it is capable of providing you with the opportunity of putting theory into practice in a useful and readily updatable way.

11 Examining office machinery and equipment

Aim of the unit

The unit provides detailed information on the sort of machinery and equipment which secretaries can expect to encounter during their career, points out principal advantages and disadvantages, and suggests appropriate selection criteria.

Specific objectives

At the end of this unit you should be able to:

1 Distinguish between different kinds of typewriter.
2 Describe the additional features present in sophisticated electronic typewriters.
3 Explain what is meant by 'single element'.
4 Identify the advantages of modern electronic typewriters.
5 Describe different types of dictation/transcription equipment.
6 Compare and contrast two types of centralised dictation system.
7 Identify the qualities of a good dictator in the preparation of audio material.
8 Provide advice for inexperienced audiotypists.
9 State the advantages and disadvantages of audiotyping for both companies and individuals.
10 Differentiate between electrically driven and electronic calculators.
11 Indicate the advantages of a printout facility on an adding machine.
12 Suggest uses to which a secretary might put an electronic calculator in the course of her work.
13 Distinguish between photocopying and duplicating.
14 State the advantages of photocopying over offset lithography and vice versa.
15 Suggest criteria on which reprographic equipment might be selected.
16 Highlight the kinds of work which a

secretary might be expected to present in bound form using an appropriate binding machine.

17 Compare and contrast spiral binding with adhesive binding.

18 Explain what is meant by 'laminating'.

19 Suggest uses to which a secretary could put a lettering machine in the course of her work.

20 Select a suitable range of modern office equipment and machinery and justify the selection.

Self-testing warm-up

1 Suggest *three* features which could make one typewriter different from another.

2 What is meant by 'dual pitch'?

3 What do you understand by 'proportional spacing', and what purpose does it serve?

4 What are the advantages of a self-correction facility on a typewriter, and are there any obvious disadvantages?

5 List *six* special features you could expect to find on an electronic typewriter.

6 When does a typewriter become a word processor?

7 When might a portable dictating machine prove useful?

8 Why is 'compatability' a word often used when discussing dictation/transcription machines?

9 What is meant by a 'tandem' dictation system?

10 What advantages does audiotyping have over shorthand?

11 What would you look for in choosing a desk-top calculator?

12 Explain briefly the principles of offset lithography.

13 What is meant by a 'flat bed' copier?

14 What is meant by an 'intelligent' or 'smart' copier?

15 Provide three reasons why an organisation might set up an internal print department.

Situation-based activities

Situation 1

Assume that you work as Typing Pool Supervisor for a small company which has recently been taken over by a large American-based corporation which has all the latest equipment. The plan is to re-equip all the offices *forthwith* with modern electronic typewriters and sophisticated audio and photocopying equipment. In the longer term this will obviously be to everyone's benefit, both Typing Pool staff and executive staff alike, but you do envisage initial 'teething' problems in the short term and feel that you had better make the position clear to both management and the staff under your supervision. Also, you must ensure that your staff has the necessary training on the new equipment.

a Write a memo to the staff under your supervision advising them of the changes. (Type if you have access to a typewriter.)

b Write a memo to be sent to your immediate superior, the Chief Administrator, outlining the problems you envisage and seeking her support during the early weeks of the new equipment. (Again type if you can.)

c Devise a suitable in-house training schedule on the use of the new equipment.

d State how you, as Supervisor, would monitor the move to the new equipment, and indicate how you would evaluate its effectiveness during the first three months of installation.

Situation 2

You work as Secretary for the boss of a small private company and your work involves a lot of complex typing requiring several carbon copies. Currently you use a standard electric typewriter which has seen better days and you would very much like to have a sophisticated electronic one such as the one you saw demonstrated at a local business efficiency exhibition last week.

Compose a memo for Mr Rogers, your boss, suggesting that he consider such an investment.

You need to 'sell' the idea to him as he is not an easy man to persuade when it comes to parting with money, although he does set store on high quality work and is anxious to create a good image for his clients. Support your request with appropriate publicity material in the form of manufacturer's literature or newspaper advertisements.

Situation 3

Your organisation has, for many years, favoured audiotyping services over shorthand writers, and it is at last being considered that such services be centralised to coincide with a move ·to new office accommodation. With this move and the introduction of a centralised system, many more staff will now make use of the facility.

a Explain in detail how you would organise the centralisation of the audiotyping services, indicating the type of system you would favour and giving reasons for your preference.
b Prepare a sheet of *clear* instructions on dictation techniques to be circulated amongst staff who will be using audio facilities for the first time.

Situation 4

You have just had a successful interview to join a new company of estate agents and valuers who are soon to open offices in your town. Part of your remit in this new post is to suggest the kind of machines and equipment you think will be required for the new offices. The staff is made up as follows:

2 Senior Partners with their own offices
2 Valuers who will share an office
You as Secretary/PA to the two partners with your own office

1 Clerk/Typist
1 Telephonist/Typist/ Receptionist — all located in an open-plan front office
1 Office Junior/ Person Friday

1 part-time Offset Litho Operator ($4\frac{1}{2}$ days a week by arrangement) located in a small machine room

The firm intends to produce all its own advertising materials, having gathered all its own information, including photographs, of properties handled.

With a view to the nature of the work, the staffing and the room allocation, prepare a comprehensive list of the kinds of machines and equipment you think will be required, giving reasons for your selections. Also comment on any additional items you think would be essential or would improve the working environment for the staff and enhance the appearance from the point of view of prospective clients and customers.

Situation 5

Your company is scrapping all its departmental copying and duplicating facilities in favour of a central Reprographics Department. A lot of doubt is being expressed throughout the offices as to the wisdom of such a decision, and many of your colleagues are decidedly against the whole idea.

You, however, feel it will be to the advantage of the office staff and that the service provided should be infinitely superior, given the range and quality of equipment scheduled for this new department. Also a lot of work which previously had to be contracted outside the company can now be produced in house. Prepare a paper which you could be asked to put forward at a staff meeting explaining the advantages of such a department as you see it from the viewpoint of a member of staff and stating the sort of work you think such a department should be able to undertake.

Situation 6

Imagine that you may select *all* new machinery and equipment for your new post as Secretary/PA to the Managing Director of an advertising agency, where your work will be very varied and where it will be expected that the standard of presentation is extremely high. Certain facilities will, of course, be on a shared basis with other secretaries, but you may assume that you have a major say as to what facilities you require, both personal and shared.

Provide details of the equipment and machinery you would like to have, justifying your selection.

Personal activities

Modern electronic office equipment is very expensive and it is unlikely that many of us will be fortunate enough to have our own, certainly in the form of electronic typewriters or word processors. However, it may be that, as has been the case with calculators (and a calculator is certainly within our reach financially), the prices will fall dramatically.

Nevertheless we can help to keep up to date with what is available by conscientiously reading and absorbing the vast quantities of literature which are published and by taking any opportunity to visit local exhibitions and demonstrations by office equipment manufacturers and suppliers.

As has been suggested earlier in this book, it is worth while to collect your own 'scrapbook' of reference material. The equipment field is an obvious example of one in which it is simple to gather useful information on all the latest machines and office equipment. This is an extremely competitive and fast moving market, and the standard of advertising material produced is very good indeed.

It would be interesting to start gathering material at the beginning of a course and to review it towards the end, noting the changes which will have taken place even in the relatively short time in which you pursue the activity.

Group activities

The activities that can be undertaken as a group or part of a group will depend very much on your imagination, the facilities you have and the time at your disposal. If, for example, you do not have very much in the way of modern office machinery and equipment, you will need to try to compensate in as many ways as you possibly can. The following are some suggestions:

1 *a* Decide on all the items of equipment that you feel you would like information about.
   b Select a range of items and divide them amongst individuals or small groups.
   c Find the addresses of the manufacturers or suppliers.
   d Compose and type polite letters to each, requesting literature on the different items of equipment.
   e When the literature arrives, decide as a group how best to use it. You may, for example, wish to prepare wall collages/information sheets utilising the details and pictures received. Alternatively you may prefer to devise a machinery and equipment index on cards and file away all the literature. Or perhaps you could decide on a combination of these two ideas.

2 Enquire into the possibility of a local firm setting up a small demonstration/exhibition within your school or college. During a quiet time of the year, or where they may wish to practise the demonstration of new equipment to a less influential audience, they may be more than willing to lay something on for you.

You may be able to put forward a more attractive proposition to a supplier by inviting representatives from local firms and industry to attend the demonstration as well as students. In this way the equipment firm has an opportunity to make useful contacts, and even one positive contact could lead to a sale which would make the day or afternoon more than worth while for them.

If you do decide to adopt this idea, be sure to plan it carefully and take the opportunity to incorporate all the organisational skills essential in making such an event a success. The following are a few points to remember:

a selection of time and place

b a format/programme for the day/afternoon
– not just a haphazard 'happening'

c sufficient advance notice to guests if any

d appropriate invitations

e formal introductions

f refreshments

g a timetable/rota where you intend opening
the event to lots of classes (it is a disaster
when everyone descends on the
demonstration at the same time)

h letters of thanks to all concerned

3 Organise a visit to modern local offices. This
can be a very interesting and worthwhile
thing to do, as not only do you see a range of
office equipment but you see it in practical
operation, which enables you to analyse
modern systems and procedures. Some
suggestions for organising the visit are as
follows:

a Try to identify personal contacts which
might exist within a group. For example,
does anyone have a relative or friend who
works somewhere which might be prepared
to host such a visit? Alternatively your
teacher/lecturer may have a contact.
Note: It is important to remember that such
an event is something of an imposition to a
firm, and goodwill cannot be called upon
too often.

b Establish the maximum numbers that an
organisation can accommodate at any one
time.

c Ask the organisation to select an
appropriate time to fit in with their normal
work pattern. This may mean rescheduling
your own classes at school/college.

d Transport problems – how will you get
there?

e Permissions – your teacher/lecturer will
require to complete certain formalities in
this respect.

f Decide in advance what you hope to gain
from the activity.

g Have some questions ready to ask.

h Someone should say a few words of thanks.

i A letter of thanks should be written to the
company and/or individual who did the
organising of the visit at the company's
end.

Practical experience

Alternatively you may be very fortunate and
have a well-equipped model office, training
office, resource workshop or similar resource in
your school or college. If so, it is up to you to
maximise your use of the facilities and be sure
that you are fully conversant with *all* the
equipment and machinery.

Any practical area is always very demanding
on the time of the teacher in that he/she can
only be in one place and with one individual or
group at a time, so be patient. However, you can
and should take the opportunity to help one
another. Explaining the operation of a piece of
equipment to someone else is a sure way of
finding out just how much you know about it
yourself.

Another thing you can usefully do is prepare
sets of instructions for the use of equipment by
others. This is never as easy as it sounds. It is so
easy to omit an essential step like where the
on/off switch is located! As an exercise this is a
very useful one and a good preparation for work
as well. Very often when companies take
delivery of new items of equipment they are
given very minimal instructions and a brief
demonstration in the use of the equipment, and
left with an often totally incomprehensible
manual to fall back on. The outcome is often the
preparation by staff of a simplified version for
the use of staff generally. Practice in such
preparations during your course will pay
dividends.

Try preparing a set of simple instructions for
a piece of equipment in your practical area.
Work in pairs and see if you can come up with a
completely logical set of instructions which
anyone can easily follow. Where appropriate
incorporate a photograph or diagram, suitably
labelled. This can greatly help clarify the
instructions. Finally, put your set of instructions

to the test. Have someone who has not used the equipment before follow them through. Ask them to be critical so that you can evaluate what you have prepared.

These are only a few suggestions of things you can do to improve your knowledge and practical application of modern office equipment and machinery. See if your group can come up with any more ideas. Remember, too, that the range of equipment around today is enormous and the likelihood of your meeting precisely the same machine when you start work is quite remote. What you need to learn are principles. Once you have done that you will find that what you learned in connection with one make of machine is readily transferable to a different model or manufacture.

12 Reviewing office technology

Aim of the unit

The unit examines the concept of the electronic office by explaining the operation and use of electronic office systems and considering developments in word and information processing and their implications for the office and for secretarial work.

Specific objectives

At the end of this unit you should be able to:

1 Give reasons for the increasing interest in office technology.
2 Define 'information'.
3 Describe the constituent parts of a word processing system.
4 Distinguish between different word processing configurations.
5 Identify the benefits of word processing.
6 Suggest reasons why organisations introduce word processing.
7 Provide selection criteria for word processing equipment.
8 Recognise and define common terms used in office technology.
9 Explain the environmental considerations in setting up a word processing facility.
10 Provide 'housekeeping' hints for word processing users.
11 Distinguish between word and information processing.
12 Recognise the potential for the introduction of information processing systems.
13 Explain what is meant by a network.
14 Compare and contrast public and private viewdata systems.
15 State the advantages of phototypesetting.
16 State the advantages of optical character recognition.
17 Explain the operation of electronic filing.
18 State the advantages and disadvantages of electronic filing.
19 Suggest likely future developments in the field of office technology.

20 Suggest ways in which the secretary's role is and will be affected by the introduction of office technology.

Self-testing warm-up

1 What does word processing hardware consist of?

2 What is meant by software?

3 What do you understand by the term 'shared resource'?

4 Explain what is meant by 'paragraph manuals'.

5 Give *six* factors you would consider when selecting a VDU.

6 Give *four* factors you would look for in a keyboard.

7 Distinguish between a daisy wheel printer and a dot matrix printer.

8 Indicate *six* general features you would expect to find in most word processing software.

9 Indicate *four* additional features you might seek in more specialised software.

10 Name *five* environmental considerations in installing word processors.

11 What is meant by 'electronic diary facility'?

12 Explain what is meant by networking.

13 Define LAN.

14 What is a modem?

15 What is teletext?

16 What is Prestel?

17 What are *three* advantages to be gained from phototypesetting?

18 Give *three* features you could expect to find as part of electronic mail.

19 What is a microwriter?

20 What is CIM?

Situation-based activities

Situation 1

Imagine that you work as a Secretary for one of the following businesses or individuals:

a a solicitor
b an employment bureau
c an estate agent
d an author
e a small theatre company

Prepare a well-considered case in support of the acquisition of a stand-alone word processor. Decide whether, given the opportunity of having one, you would opt for a dedicated system or a microcomputer with word processing software. Supply justifications for your decision.

Got some spare time? Well, why not select an alternative and go through the whole process again?!

Situation 2

Assume that you work for a local authority or your local council offices and that you are a member of a working party set up to investigate the possibility of gradually introducing word processing into your offices, beginning in six months' time. The working party has a remit which covers the following:

a an investigation into the work of the offices
b recommendations as to which areas of the work would be suited to word processing and the order in which the sections ought to make the transition
c the selection of equipment
d the siting of equipment and all environmental and health aspects associated with the installation
e discussions with trade unions
f the appointment of a Word Processing Supervisor
g the selection and training of staff
h the evaluation of the system after installation

Your tasks are as follows:

a Describe, in detail, how your working party would go about investigating the content and nature of work in different departments, and highlight any problems you would expect to encounter.

b What sort of work will tend to lend itself most readily to word processing, and why?

c Prepare detailed specifications of the features you would look for:

   i in VDUs
   ii in keyboards
   iii in printers
   iv in software

d Draw a room plan for the installation of *six* word processing work stations. Suggest a colour scheme and detail *all* additional equipment/supplies you would envisage being required. Also indicate any precautions you would take in connection with health aspects.

e Outline the basis of your discussions with relevant trade unions and indicate any problems which you can anticipate in advance of such meetings.

f Prepare an advertisement for a Word Processing Supervisor and draw up a job description for the post.

g Indicate in a memo to the Training Department the types of staff selection and training which will be required prior to and following the installation.

h Suggest ways in which the new system can be evaluated in the early months following its installation.

Situation 3

Your organisation has been using word processing systems for several years now, and you have been asked by your boss to represent the company at a local school where you have been asked to talk to a group of secretarial students on word processing. You have to assume that they can all type but that none of them knows anything at all about word processing, and they certainly have no WP equipment.

a Prepare notes for your talk.

b Draw up *three* simple diagrams which you will use to support your talk.

c Devise a brief handout (one side of A4 paper)

giving some basic information which will substantiate what you had to say.

Situation 4

Your office junior has arrived in your office having attended day release classes at the local college of further education yesterday afternoon. She is absolutely full of enthusiasm about a word processing system which she saw demonstrated there, but has a list of terminology which the salesman used during the demonstration and which she did not understand. Can you help her? Here are her problems:

a He talked about 'booting' the system.
b He referred to 'buffer storage'.
c He talked about 'formatting'.
d He referred to something called a 'modem'.
e He mentioned something about 'reverse video'.
f What did he mean by 'scrolling'?
g What does it mean if a system is upgradable?
h I can't remember what CPU stood for.
i Would I be correct in thinking he talked about 'library documents'? If so, what are they?
j Also there was something he referred to that sounded as if he was talking about football. Can you think what it might have been? If you can, will you explain it to me?

Now let's see just how well versed *you* are on the terminology.

Situation 5

Up to this time all your department's records have been kept using traditional filing equipment and procedures. It is proposed that you will, in the next six months, transfer all records on to electronic media with a view to increasing the effectiveness of information retrieval and update and improving security of confidential records.

a What initial problems will you be likely to experience with such a changeover?

b Indicate how you would tackle
implementation.
c What differences would there be in indexing?
d What are the advantages of operating a
database management system?

Situation 6

Assume that you are well versed with the
principles and practice of word processing, and
that your organisation, which has been in the
front line in office technology, is having the
latest information processing equipment
installed throughout the offices in your building.
The new equipment has additional facilities to
those you have already used. They include the
following:

a electronic mail
b electronic diary facility
c electronic in-tray
d viewdata
e voice annotation facility

Imagine that you are writing to a colleague from
another branch of the organisation yet to install
the new equipment. Tell her about your new
'toy', and explain how you think it will work and
what uses you expect to be able to make of these
new sophisticated facilities.

Situation 7

As the General Manager's Secretary you have
been using a word processor for a few years now.
However, the company is moving over to
computer-based systems more and more as it
progresses towards a totally integrated office. As
part of an electronic office induction programme
the Personnel Officer has asked you to speak on
'housekeeping'. He would like you to include the
general care of the hardware, reference to disc
handling, labelling, copying and general storage
and back-up. Prepare a brief talk and state how
you would illustrate the talk and bring it to life
for your audience.

Situation 8

You are a member of a word and information

processing society. Next month's meeting is one
at which you and a selection of other members
have been asked to talk about your own
experiences with word processing. You have
decided to talk about setting up a mail shot as
you do a lot of this in your work.

Prepare your talk – in full, as it is possible that
a transcript of it may be requested by your
company afterwards.

Also required for next month's meeting are
suggestions for future topics which members
would like to have covered during next season's
meetings. As this is such a fast moving area of
knowledge there are many relatively unexplored
avenues which you think might be worth
including in such a programme. Suggest *six*
possibilities.

Personal activities

As with Unit 11 it is not easy to suggest things
you can actually do using sophisticated
technological equipment without knowing
something about you and where you live, not to
mention the interests of your family. However,
you may have access to a teletext TV set; even
where you have an ordinary set, selected
material (often news information or details of
future programmes) is shown at times when no
set programme is scheduled, and this is one way
of actually experiencing technology at work.

Home computers

You may, of course, already have a computer in
your home, but you will probably find yourself
competing for computer time with other
enthusiasts in your family, such is the growing
popularity of such equipment. Anyway, take
whatever opportunities you can get to gain
familiarity with this type of equipment – even if
it means playing computer games! Mind you,
where you possess existing keyboard skills you
may find yourself in demand as you will be
infinitely better equipped to key in program
data.

Television programmes

Be sure to preview the TV papers. There are often programmes which will be of interest, and unless you study the programme guides carefully it is easy to miss them.

Reading

As mentioned in Unit 11, a lot of useful information can be gained simply through reading and becoming familiar with the terminology. There is certainly no shortage of material; the problem, in fact, is to be selective. Remember the advice about reading given in Part I.

Exhibitions/demonstrations

Information technology (IT) is very much the thing of the moment and exhibitions are held regularly. There are also many established IT centres throughout the country where you can 'drop in' at any time, look around and seek the advice and help of experts.

Open access

Some colleges offer what is termed an 'open access' facility where you can book in for a series of what are often self-paced, self-taught sessions. You are given access to a computer terminal and using a specially prepared self-teach package, have the opportunity to work your way through a range of simple programs. Teaching and technical staff are on hand to help you with any problems.

Practical activities

The following are three practical activities in word processing and office technology. Where you have access to word processing and viewdata facilities, put the exercises into practice. (In some instances you may simulate the activity equally well using a typewriter.)

1 Assume that your company has recently invested in word processing equipment. You, as one of the secretaries who will use the equipment, have been asked to join a team which will ultimately produce a reference manual which will be used by all personnel in an attempt to standardise formats for all letters, memoranda, reports and business forms, as well as establish a paragraph manual to which all staff may refer in preparing business correspondence.

a Using a word processing terminal, *experiment* with layouts for the following:

A5 letters	notices of meetings
A4 letters	agendas
memoranda	minutes
short reports	stationery
lengthy formal reports	requisitions
telephone message forms	invoices

Enjoy yourself – don't be afraid to let yourself go. Be creative and imaginative. Remember how easily you can alter what you do!

b i Suggest typical pieces of text/sentences/ short paragraphs/longer standard paragraphs which might frequently be used in the preparation of business correspondence.

ii Come up with suitable suggestions for ways in which they might readily be referred to in a paragraph manual for ease of retrieval in a word processing routine. For example:

Dear Sir might be abbreviated to 'ds' your company name might be appropriately reduced (practise with your school or college!)

The possibilities are endless, so let your imagination flow.

2 Imagine that you are part of a team of secretaries training authors within your organisation to make the best use of word pro-

cessing. If you have access to a word processor, use it to produce these tasks:

a Devise a list of say ten pointers which could be given to prospective authors to help them prepare material for word processing so that operators will readily understand their requirements.

b Devise a business letter and type it up. On it, write in examples of the following alterations, using marks understood by word processing operators:

capital letters
underscoring
centring
emboldening
new paragraph
change the layout eg from blocked to indented
run on into same paragraph
transpose letters
transpose words
alter page arrangements in terms of paragraph order
change the margins

Where you have access to a word processor, prepare the text *before and after* the alterations.

3 Where you have access to viewdata facilities such as Prestel, find the following information:

a times of flights from London Heathrow to Barcelona, and the cost
b whether any inoculations are currently required for travel to India
c the current rate of exchange of sterling to the following:

the dollar
the franc
the mark
the peseta
the lira

d the weather forecast for your area of the country

e members of the Cabinet – who are they, and what positions do they hold?
f the current *Financial Times* (FT) Index
g information on educational courses for secretaries
h whether you can order wine by Access
i what is currently playing at London West End theatres
j sporting fixtures for the coming weekend
k road conditions

Note: Where you do not have access to this equipment it is, of course, possible to find all this information from more conventional sources. What are they in each case?

Group activities

Here again, activities depend on the time, facilities and imagination available. Anything relating to information technology and the electronic office of the future is usually more enjoyable as a shared experience. So one piece of advice is to pool your ideas and your resources. You'll get a lot more out of it that way.

Once again, where you may not have much in the way of resources, either physical or financial, use your ingenuity to effect. Write off for information. Build up a library of information. Visit exhibitions. Try to establish links with users. Join associations. Look out for suitable TV programmes (your school or college may be able to video them, if they are geared towards the education market or they have the appropriate licence). Watching as a group is more fun.

Hire of films

This is not always as expensive as it may seem, and where several groups can be involved and have the benefit the cost may be broken down and shared out.

Suggestions for games

Games provide a way to get to grips with the jargon of technology.

Take a list of twenty items – there is a glossary at the end of Unit 12 in *Secretarial Procedures*. Opposite each item place three definitions. Only one will be correct. Type out the material and duplicate or photocopy the sheets with the terms and the suggested definitions. Circulate the sheets. Decide on a time limit. Players should select their answer, namely 1, 2 or 3. See who gets the most correct.

Alternatively you can be a bit more ambitious and form two teams for 'Call My Bluff'. In case you are unfamiliar with this popular TV panel game, here briefly is how it goes. There are two teams with three in each team, and a chairperson. The chairperson reads out the word (or in this instance, phrase). One team puts forward three possible definitions for the other team to consider, only one of which is correct – hence 'true' or 'bluff'. The other team must decide which member of the opposing team is telling the truth. A good end of term game for you to play, perhaps?

Another suggestion involves the same sort of set up as described for 'Call My Bluff', but this time the chairperson has all the correct terms and definitions typed on cards. He puts the questions to the teams, one at a time, and tests them on their ability to supply a satisfactory answer. If they are correct they gain three points for their team. If they are wrong the question is passed to the opposing team for a two-mark bonus. And so the game continues.

Part III　Crossword puzzles

The crossword puzzles which make up this part of the book have been devised to serve as general revision.

Some of the clues you will find strikingly obvious, whilst others may seem somewhat cryptic. All the answers, however, are to be found within the text of *Secretarial Procedures*.

Solutions are provided at the end of this part. However, do persevere and try to complete the puzzles yourself before rushing to the answers – they all seem easy then!

Puzzle 1

Across

1 A cause for concern – it should come
first (6)

4 You don't need a tool to do the office
variety (6)

7 Abbreviation for anagram of game (1)

9 The brain of the system (3)

10 It happens at elections (6)

12 To set down in writing, or song
perhaps? (6)

14 To plot (3)

15 Abbreviation for Latin words used for
your personal profile (2)

16 Equal to 8 bits (4)

17 Some believe that technology will do
this – sell kid (anagram) (7)

19 Interrogate for a job (9)

22 Samuel Pepys was famous for his (5)

23 You don't want your statement to
appear this way (3)

25 The other half of visual perhaps? (5)

26 Things to be done (6)

28 Usually located near the door (9)

32 Trivial (5)

33 Not a popular additive (3)

34 Published daily (10)

Down

2 A common classification (12)

3 Said to combine the speed of one
thing with the authority of another (5)

5 Used when referring to a thing   (2)

6 Observe – every meeting should have one   (6)

8 'Bell, . . . and candle' (E A Poe)   (4)

11 A game with typewriter connections?   (4)

13 The opposite of Cr   (5)

18 A collection of 8 down   (7)

20 The popular abbreviation for the focal point of a work station   (3)

21 The second part of a well-known book of reference – nothing to do with the medical profession!   (3)

24 Translate in computer language   (6)

27 Could be musical or shorthand   (5)

29 Secretary/??   (2)

30 Spoken   (4)

31 The big chief perhaps?   (2)

32 An edible chart?   (3)

Puzzle 2

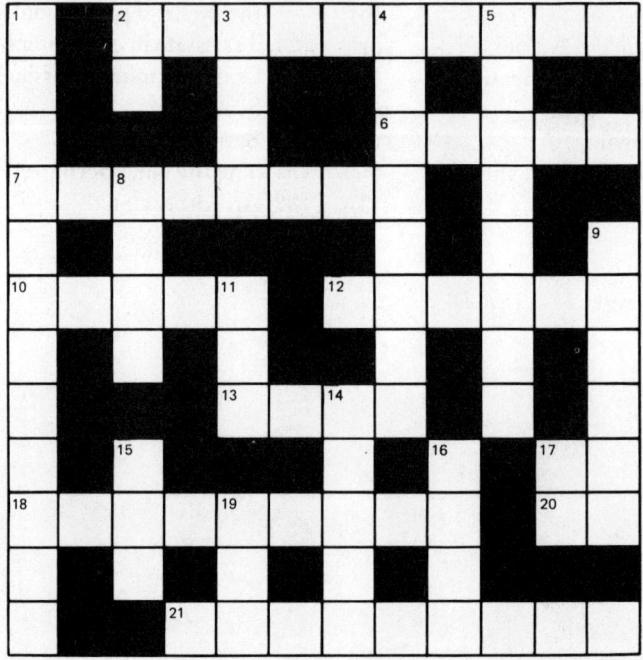

Across

2	We have Alexander Graham Bell to thank for them	(10)
6	Proportion	(5)
7	It's usually a QWERTY one	(8)
10	A form of transport	(5)
12	The other part of 19 down	(6)
13	'. . . waits for no man'	(4)
17	A promoting area of work	(2)
18	Often preferable to a loan	(9)
20	A lower animal perhaps?	(2)
21	A formal account	(9)

Down

1	Found in all offices of the future	(4,8)
2	How often do you look at it?	(2)
3	Identifying symbols	(4)
4	Nothing floppy about the durability of this	(8)
5	No longer just associated with the media	(8)
8	Twelve months	(4)
9	Sell abroad	(6)
11	Used in fishing	(3)
14	Intended	(5)
15	Perhaps to become a redundant writing tool?	(3)
16	Time (anagram)	(4)
17	The sixteenth letter of the Greek alphabet	(2)
19	To do with Morse code? (see also 12 across)	(3)

Puzzle 3

Across

3 A smaller version of 3 down (6)

5 A structure by which to reach decisions? (9)

8 The secretary and her boss should be one (4)

11 Restrain (7)

14 The minimum needed (6)

15 Relate formally (6)

16 A long time (4)

18 A group of persons (5)

19 Each (5)

20 See 25 across

25 Handling information (see also 20 across) (4,10)

26 Your course? (11)

Down

1 A VDU has one (6)

2 Information technology (2)

3 Found on a piano (8)

4 Affirmative (3)

6 A legal aspect – dealing with wrongs (4)

7 Top twenty? (6)

9 Diary (7)

10 Singing well? In good form? (7)

12 Flashing signal (6)

13 Is said to broaden the mind (6)

17 In-house communiques (5)

20 Call aloud for (4)

21 Revise (4)

22 Asterisk (4)

23 A target in sport (4)

24 Connected with microfilm (3)

Puzzle 4

Across

1	Those in charge perhaps?	(9)
4	A trick (see 18 down)	(3)
7	Yearly	(6)
8	Not good	(3)
9	Digital to analogue	(5)
12	One way to secure information	(8)
14	Half a score	(3)
16	A house-trained computer?	(3)
17	No need to buy it – you can still see it in 27 across	(6)
20	The press represents one aspect	(5)
21	Item (anagram)	(4)
23	Glance through quicky	(4)
24	Less than gross	(3)
25	A popular way to keep fit	(3)
26	A high technology abbreviation	(2)
27	See 17 across	(2)
28	Held once a year	(3)

Down

1	Non-speaking	(4)
2	You should also do this with small print	(4)
3	A WP system arrangement	(13)
5	A printer's instruction	(2)
6	Tower (anagram)	(5)
9	You'd need one to find buried treasure	(3)
10	Every letter should show this	(4)
11	A long informal note?	(10)
13	The abbreviation of the moment perhaps?	(2)
14	An air of finality? Often linked to 1 down	(8)
15	It appears on your salary slip	(2)
18	The first half of 4 across	(3)
19	A shaft of light	(5)
22	Make a cut	(4)

Puzzle 5

Across

1 Introduce to work (6)
3 Method (6)
6 An abbreviation seen on shipping documents (3)
7 Top personnel (9)
9 They ring or bleep (6)
10 A bit more than just word handling (abbreviation) (2)
13 Work (4)
14 There isn't time to become one of these in an office (10)
16 A printing liquid (see also 5 down) (3)
18 Associated with computers not sheep! (3)
19 Type – not tar! (5)
20 It can become addictive (2)
21 Pass down authority and responsibility (8)

Down

1 Short form facts (4)
2 Copy a soundtrack (3)
4 A brief form of record (see also 10 down) (5,5)
5 Engines which contribute to sophisticated reprographics? (see also 15 across) (4)
7 Printed reports of Parliamentary debates (7)
8 Published annually (8)
10 See 4 down (5)
11 Not only found in Egypt (7)
12 Can be handled electronically (7)
15 A concert perhaps? (4)
17 Observe a musical symbol (4)

Puzzle 6

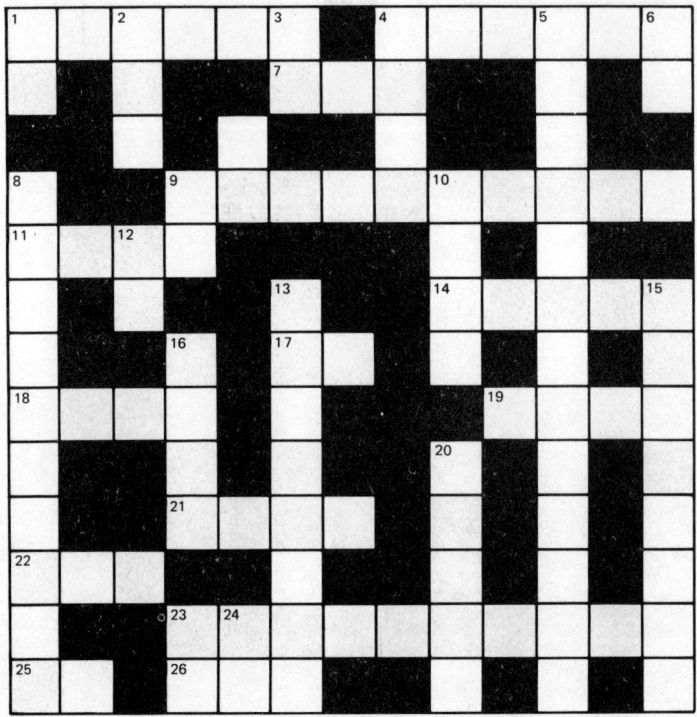

Across

1 Not private	(6)
4 Between a few	(6)
7 Technical name for WP screen	(3)
9 Methods	(10)
11 They help with directions	(4)
14 The science of reasoning	(5)
17 See 13 down	
18 Spoken	(4)
19 A tropical tree	(4)
21 Could be 16 down	(4)
22 Finish	(3)
23 You won't find these small creatures in your fish tank!	(10)
25 Compulsive viewing?	(2)
26 Besides	(3)

Down

1 A top level secretarial title	(2)
2 A binary digit	(3)
3 Popular alternative to an application form	(2)
4 Certain	(4)
5 Duplicating forms a part of it	(13)
6 It was around before word processing	(2)
8 See 13 down	
9 An addendum to a letter	(2)
10 Not shiny	(4)
12 The afternoon or the resident of number ten	(2)
13 Legal basis for work (and 17 across, 8 down)	(8,2,10)
15 Soon every home may have one	(8)
16 An O & M interest (see 21 across)	(4)
20 Trial run	(5)
23 Belonging to me	(2)
24 That is (abbreviation)	(2)

Answers to crossword puzzles

Puzzle 1

Across

1 safety
4 filing
7 M
9 CPU
10 voting
12 record
14 map
15 CV
16 byte
17 deskill
19 interview
22 diary
23 red
25 audio
26 agenda
28 reception
32 petty
33 VAT
34 newspapers

Down

2 alphabetical
3 telex
5 it
6 notice
8 book
11 golf
13 debit
18 library
20 VDU
21 who
24 decode
27 notes
29 PA
30 oral
31 MD
32 pie

Puzzle 2

Across

2 telephones
6 ratio
7 keyboard
10 train
12 matrix
13 time
17 PR
18 overdraft
20 it
21 statement

Down

1 work stations
2 TV
3 logo
4 hardware
5 networks
8 year
9 export
11 net
14 meant
15 pen
16 item
17 pi
19 dot

Puzzle 3

Across

3 keypad
5 committee
8 team
11 control
14 quorum
15 report
16 ages
18 panel
19 every
20 processing
25 word
26 secretarial

Down

1 screen
2 IT
3 keyboard
4 yes
6 tort
7 charts
9 journal
10 invoice
12 cursor
13 travel
17 memos
20 page
21 edit
22 star
23 goal
24 COM

Puzzle 5

Across

1 induct
3 system
6 FOB
7 hierarchy
9 phones
10 IP
13 job
14 daydreamer
16 ink
18 RAM
19 pitch
20 TV
21 delegate

Down

1 info
2 dub
4 strip
5 jets
7 *Hansard*
8 yearbook
10 index
11 pyramid
12 mailing
15 PROM
17 note

Puzzle 4

Across

1 directors
4 con
7 annual
8 bad
9 modem
12 viewdata
14 ten
16 Pet
17 rental
20 media
21 time
23 scan
24 net
25 jog
26 LAN
27 TV
28 AGM

Down

1 dumb
2 read
3 configuration
5 NP
6 wrote
9 map
10 date
11 memorandum
13 WP
14 terminal
15 NI
18 *nem*
19 laser
22 edit

Puzzle 6

Across

1 public
4 shared
7 VDU
9 procedures
11 maps
14 logic
17 of
18 oral
19 palm
21 work
22 end
23 microfiche
25 TV
26 yet

Down

1 PA
2 bit
3 CV
4 sure
5 reprographics
6 DP
8 employment
9 PS
10 dull
12 PM
13 contract
15 computer
16 flow
20 draft
23 my
24 ie

Part IV   Preparing for examinations

Introduction

In Part I, I talked about studying and how you can learn to study effectively. Similarly, with a little consideration and determination you can better equip yourself to tackle any examination and go a long way towards ensuring your success.

Preparation for examinations should be an ongoing activity from the time you embark upon the course. To achieve good results – and you should always aim to do more than scrape a pass – revision must form a regular part of your study routine from the very beginning. This is another reason for acquiring the official syllabus of the examining board at the start (some useful addresses are given at the back of the book); you will then have the whole course set out before you and it is easier to monitor your progress through it. Remember, however, that your teacher or lecturer is unlikely to approach the syllabus in the exact order in which it is presented by the examination board.

As your course progresses you should be able to look back over the syllabus, examining the ideas you have already met, testing your existing knowledge, refreshing your mind and generally assessing your understanding to date.

Where you adopt this sort of strategy there will never be any desperate need to try to cram all revision into the last minute. Research into memory indicates that early revision is important; it will make later material easier for you to learn, as there will be a better understanding of what has gone before.

Revision timetable

As examinations draw near you will need to adopt a more systematic approach to your revision. In the last five or six weeks a special revision timetable should be prepared, listing the topics you need to revise and the order in which you intend to tackle them.

Just as for your PSP (personal study

programme), you will need to pace yourself and space out your revision, not forgetting to leave some time for rest and recreation – especially during the last few days! You don't want to go into the examinations exhausted before you begin! You might consider using a Gantt chart to map out this sort of revision programme. Draw up an ideal model and see how closely you are able to stick to it in practice!

Study syndicates

Some students find it invaluable to form a sort of study syndicate with fellow students for revision. Obviously you will need to get along well together working as a group and be prepared to adhere closely to your work schedule for the venture to be successful. This requires immense discipline, but the benefits to be gained from the shared experience may make it worth while.

One point that perhaps needs to be stressed is that group working will only have maximum effect where the group is formed early in a course of study. Such groups operate to a large extent on a mutual self-help basis in that group members may use one another as 'sounding boards' for their ideas and problems.

One advantage is that it may help you to be more objective about your course. When you work alone there will always be areas of study which you will tend to favour and perhaps devote more time to than is necessary. Where you are revising as part of a group, other people's preferences will differ from yours and consequently it is more likely that you will achieve better overall syllabus coverage.

As examinations approach you can, as individuals, attempt questions from past papers and circulate your answers around the group for criticism and comment. When you take part in this sort of activity you must be prepared to offer constructive (not destructive) criticism to your friends as well as accept criticism when it comes your way.

You will find yourself adopting the role of 'teacher' for the topics you enjoy and feel confident about; it is surprising how valuable it can be, in achieving clarity in your own thinking, to attempt to explain points to others. Conversely you will tend to fall into the student/learner role for the topics you find more difficult to grasp and absorb, and here again the explanations of one of your fellow students may remove the mystery from something which has confused or troubled you all year!

Specific pointers to aid revision

One thing that is, I think, abundantly clear to all who prepare for examinations is the do-it-yourself nature of the activity. Ultimately, irrespective of how much tuition, advice and shared experience you have had during the year, it will be up to you and you alone when it comes to the examination. Nobody will be there to advise you and assist during the examination. Nobody can help jog you along by offering words of consolation and encouragement. The experience – and for some students it can be a traumatic one – will be yours alone, and it will fall to you alone to do your best. This you can help ensure by being as well prepared as possible.

The previous comments have been of a general nature. There are more specific things that will help you to maximise the time you spend revising (particularly when you have more than one subject) and to feel more confident about tackling the examination when the day actually arrives. The following are a few suggestions:

1 *Examination format*   Be sure that you are fully conversant with the form that the examination will take (see later).
2 *Examination techniques*   You need to master not only the factual information inherent in the study of the subject but also the techniques required to satisfy the examiner, ie how to tackle the paper.
3 *Answering practice*   You need to practice writing answers for questions from past

papers. Where the examination format is basically traditional (ie you are required to answer so many questions from a certain number in a given period) it is essential that you know how much you are physcially capable of writing in the given time. And you need to practise!

4 *Materials*   Practise using the same sort of materials as you are likely to get in the examination, ie use A4 broad lined paper with an inch margin on either side and write with a pen rather than a pencil. Whether you prefer to use a traditional pen with ink, a ballpoint or a fibre tip will be a matter for you to decide. However, it is worth while experimenting, from the point of view both of ease of writing and of the end product: which is the easiest and clearest to read?

5 *Time yourself*   How much can you write in half an hour? As a benchmark, the average, mentally agile student of any subject, writing clearly in average-sized handwriting (about ten words per line) should be capable of filling approximately two sides of A4 paper in half an hour.

6 *Quantity or quality*   It is important to appreciate that what you write must be what is required to answer the question. There is no point in being able to write two sides in half an hour if the content is irrelevant, incomprehensible and repetitive rubbish!

7 *Reading*   Practise reading the questions and interpreting their requirements. The most common fault of all students at all levels and in all types of examination is *careless reading*, resulting in *failure to answer the question.*

8 *What are the examiners looking for?*   Time spent going through past papers will help considerably in establishing this (something you can usefully do in a group). There are only so many ways a topic can be viewed, and consequently only so many ways a question can be set – and therefore only so many answers! Every question will require some indication of factual subject knowledge in the answer. It is a question of identifying the appropriate slant and structuring your response in a logical, well-presented sequence.

9 *Making the most out of your notes*   Good notes really come into their own during revision. Where they are detailed, you will be well advised to begin to condense them. The use of highlighting pens can be very useful as an aid to this activity.

10 *Revision cards*   Eventually you should be in a position to reduce your notes on to manageable cards, containing the essential items of information. These may take the form of key words, dates, names – in fact anything that will cue your recall of the more detailed material in the notes. Cards are useful in that they may be easily carried around and consulted at odd moments, eg on the bus or in the train. You should be able eventually to visualise the entire contents of a card in your mind's eye: think how useful that could be in the examination room!

11 *To select or not to select?*   This is a question which you must consider carefully when it comes to deciding what exactly you are going to revise. Can you really afford to ignore a syllabus item in its entirety? This will depend to a large extent on the structure and format of the examination, ie how many questions you need to answer and how extensive is the choice.

12 *Using a cassette recorder*   Sometimes it can be worthwhile reading your notes or extracts from your textbook on to a cassette so that you can play it back later. This can help you consolidate, and does reduce the pressure of continually reading and rereading.

13 *Check the teacher/lecturer's written comments on assessed work*   Teachers and lecturers often spend many hours reading through your work. Where they have offered comments you will be well advised to take heed of them, and they should certainly be useful for revision.

14 *Checking your own notes made during class revision*   One particularly good time to

make notes in class is during the run-up to an examination when you are probably going through past papers as a group. You should make notes (on the actual question papers if they are yours) whilst the questions are being discussed, and pay particular attention to any points which the teacher may add.

Note: A selection of actual past examination questions is included at the end of each unit in *Secretarial Procedures*. Why not use them to try out your revision techniques?

Past examination papers

As mentioned above, it will be usual for you to consider past examination papers as an integral part of your school or college course. Most teachers will spend at least some time with classes examining past papers and offering advice on how to tackle certain questions. You may even be set a past examination paper by way of a mock or dress rehearsal prior to your actual examination.

However, should time be very restricted on your course, or should your teacher have very limited access to past papers, it will be well worth your while to write off to the exam board yourself and secure some past copies. Most syllabuses from exam boards provide a list of the past papers available, together with the costs.

The study of a few previous papers will provide you with some indication of the overall syllabus coverage of the examination and will give you a 'feel' for the way questions tend to be set. Also, where you identify questions with which you would have experienced difficulty, you will know to which areas you need to devote more revision time! Where you have started to revise early enough you will be in a position to ask the advice of your teacher about a question that has caused you problems. Similarly, many teachers will ask students to suggest any topics they would like to revise in class time prior to the examination. The fact that suggestions are

not usually particularly forthcoming is not in most instances an indication of supreme confidence on the part of the students! Rather it is a lack of awareness of the areas of difficulty.

Types of question and examination formats

I have already recommended the acquisition of official syllabuses. This is really essential to familiarise yourself with the requirements of the examination. Obviously different techniques require to be applied to different sorts of questions and to different sorts of examination, and it is important that you are well versed in the techniques of the examinations you are going to attempt.

Let me elaborate a little on what I mean by describing a few different question types and examining the format of different examinations.

Traditional examination paper

Here students are required to answer say five out of eight or ten questions. Students are free to select any five questions of their own. Each question will carry equal marks, so it may be assumed that equal time should be allocated to each question – possibly half an hour per answer.

Sometimes there may be a compulsory question followed by say any four others, whilst on other occasions the paper may be divided into sections with specific instructions as to the number of questions to be attempted from each section. In the latter it is important to be completely clear in your own mind of the options open to you.

In these sorts of examination the answers will basically be of an essay type, which means that they should be well structured with a good introduction, the development of the argument or theme, and a suitable conclusion. Incidentally, never waste valuable time rewriting the actual question. It is sufficient to number your answers clearly to correspond with the numbering of the question paper.

You will be well advised to undertake a brief essay plan before you actually commit pen to paper in the final format. Sequence is important and you want to try to present your points in a logical order. Also you want to include as many relevant points as you can to substantiate your answer. Advance planning will help you to achieve a good result.

Two-part examinations

Many examinations are structured in that students are required to attempt two quite separate parts. Part I may take the form of short answer questions or perhaps an objective test of some kind. The idea here is to provide you with a good opportunity to demonstrate your syllabus knowledge over a wide range of material, even though the treatment required is superficial. A time allocation is usually stipulated, eg 'You are advised to spend no longer than 40 minutes on this section.' Be sure that you follow the advice. If you really know your subject matter well you may find that you can actually complete this part in less than the 40 minutes and so gain some extra time to deal with Part II. This part will be in the form of full-blown questions along the traditional lines previously indicated.

Question types

Questions can be posed in a variety of different ways, and it is vital that you assess them carefully to ascertain *precisely* what is required. A good way to do this is to look for the *key verb* in the sentence. This will help indicate the sort of answer you will be required to provide. Here are some common verbs used in examination questions:

describe	analyse
explain	indicate
define	criticise
compare	contrast
comment	discuss
justify	provide

Obviously if you are specifically asked to 'compare and contrast', and you simply write around the subject, little credit will be given for your answer. Similarly, if you 'describe' when you were asked to 'analyse', you have failed to answer the question.

Sometimes questions may be in two parts. In such instance be sure that you have tackled both parts. If there is an (a) and a (b) be sure that your answer is presented in such a way as to indicate clearly which part of your answer refers to (a) and which part to (b).

Where questions are broken down for mark allocation (eg the first part is for three marks, the second for five marks and the third for twelve marks), be sure that your answer is appropriately weighted towards these marks.

Follow any instructions implicitly. Where a question asks for something specific (eg 'give *three* examples . . .'), provide it (give *three* not four or five!) Where you are asked to write in so many words, do so. Do not write more or less. Where you are asked to write a report, write a report using the recognised conventions of report writing. Where you are asked to provide notes, provide notes – not an essay! These points may seem obvious, but it is amazing how many students fail to do what they are asked!

Situation-based questions

It is becoming increasingly popular, particularly in secretarial examinations, for examiners to devise questions around situations. Here it is important that you answer the questions in a manner appropriate to the situations described. Sometimes the preamble to the question will be lengthy and even complex, and you may well need to read the question a few times to absorb the atmosphere and get the feel of the situation. A highlighting pen is useful for this sort of question, as it will help focus your attention on any aspect of the situation which is particularly significant and relevant to the way in which you will choose to tackle your answer.

Situation-based examinations

An extension of the situation-based question is the situation-based examination, eg RSA Secretarial Duties Stage II. Here you need to adopt a role at the very beginning and, with the role firmly in mind, carry out the 'in-tray' assignments which follow. The type of organisation for which you are supposed to work will strongly influence the way in which you tackle certain tasks, and you will be expected to accurately reflect the situation. You need to refer back constantly to the rubric to ensure that you are still 'in character' and on the 'right set'. It is all too easy to jump on the general theme of a question and simply trot out everything you know about it regardless of the situation you are supposed to be in. This can be a difficult activity, particularly where you have no real work experience to draw from, but practice does help. Also it is important that you 'play the game' and enter into the spirit of the situation for the purposes of the examination. There is no point in saying afterwards that you would never have done such a thing if you were in the job described! You must 'wear the appropriate hat' even if it seems like a funny one to you. Only that way can you hope to produce the sort of response to the situation which the examiner is looking for.

Priority questions

In RSA Secretarial Duties Stage II you are also required to indicate a *priority* task. This is usually reasonably obvious but it may on occasions require that you give the matter a little more thought. Try to be realistic. What would you do first in the situation described, and why?

Reading time

Many examinations provide reading time prior to the actual writing time allocated. In most instances this will be around ten minutes, and during that time you are usually allowed to make notes, although not actually to commence writing your answers. Reading time is extremely valuable and you should make the best use you can of it, making any notes, underlining or highlighting important points, perhaps determining which questions you will answer if you have a choice and in which order you will attempt them.

Advice for the day of the examination

1 Try to avoid 'previewing' on the way to the examination. What you haven't revised is not worth considering at this stage.
2 Try to avoid discussing the examination with other candidates. They are only likely to depress you by mentioning areas you have skimmed or omitted totally in your revision.
3 Arrive in the examination room in good time, preferably after a good night's sleep and something to eat. If it is important to you where you sit, and you think there may be a choice, be sure to arrive extra early!
4 If you are able to select your seat, choose a place where you will feel comfortable and where you will encounter the least distraction.
5 Try to relax.
6 When you get the paper *read* it through very carefully, making notes in the reading time if permitted to do so.
7 Do not be in a frantic rush to start – take your time and try to get the feel of the paper.
8 Be sure that you know how many questions you need to answer in the time allowed and allocate your time accordingly. Budget your time according to the number of questions and the marks awarded for them (if these are made known to you). Obviously this is more easily done where each question carries an equal number of marks. It is useful to actually make a note of the times at which you expect to complete your different questions.
9 When reading the questions, make sure that you know what the examiner is asking for. Don't make the mistake of seeing a familiar

phrase and leaping in and answering what you think the question may be about or what you wish it was about! Try to be objective and not to misread questions.

10 Be sure that you have understood the instructions. One of the most common errors made by candidates is failure to do what is asked.

11 When you have selected your questions, make some brief notes or a skeleton outline before you actually start writing your answer. Try to identify the main relevant points which you should include in your answer. Also allow for a bit of free association. Let your mind be open to any possible ideas which you think of, even though you may wish to discard some of them later. Jot down on paper everything that comes into mind, and then *plan* your answer from your notes. You want your answer not to come out like a rag-bag of thoughts and ideas, but to have an organised and logical structure; so it is necessary to plan.

12 Keep referring back to the question as you write to make sure that you are still answering it! If you feel that you are becoming bogged down, losing the thread or running out of inspiration, leave a big space and go to the next question. You may be able to return to it later.

13 Keep an eye on the time. Check periodically with your watch or the clock in the room.

14 Don't make the common mistake of spending too much time on your best question and consequently running short of time with the others.

15 Pay attention to spelling and grammar. Avoid misspelling words which appear on the question paper. This is inexcusable!

16 Try to be concise. There is nothing to be gained from excessive waffle.

17 Above all, write legibly.

18 If you manage to complete the paper before the time is up, don't rush out of the room. Read through your paper. You just might spot an obvious error or omission or even have a last-minute flash of inspiration.

19 If you do find that you are running out of time, at least try to get the main points down on paper – without the detail.

20 Avoid post-mortems afterwards. They rarely help.

In this part I have set out to provide you with some advice in preparing for examinations, based on my experiences in taking examinations and on the advice I have offered my students over the years. As I have stressed, when you come down to it examinations are very personal experiences – and experiences most of us would much rather do without! However, in today's competitive world they are a fact of life, and we owe it to ourselves to do everything we can to ease the process. Much of this depends on adequate and appropriate preparation, designed to suit our personal needs and circumstances. So take time and give the matter some extra thought. Careful planning and preparation usually pays dividends. Good luck!

Useful addresses

The London Chamber of Commerce and
Industry
Marlowe House
Station Road
SIDCUP
Kent DA15 7BJ

Pitman Examinations Institute
Catteshall Manor
GODALMING
Surrey GU7 1UU

Royal Society of Arts Examinations Board
(Publications)
Murray Road
ORPINGTON
Kent BR5 3RB